Tweet

FOR

Twat

Tweet for Twat:
How Social Networks, Media and Technology Affect Modern-Day Relationships and Dating

Miami, Florida 33131

Cover Art by Mordecai Ray

First Printing, March 29, 2013
ISBN-13: 978-0-9891672-0-8
ISBN-10: 0989167208
Library of Congress Control Number: 2013905183

Tweet

FOR

Twat

How Social Networks, Media and Technology Affect

Modern-Day Relationships and Dating

CLAUDIA VERSAILLES

DEDICATION

To Greg Paul— my motivator and my biggest supporter. You believe in me even when I stop believing in myself. Thank you for being one of my blessings. My soul appreciates you.

Website: www.Tweet4Twat.com
Twitter: @Tweet4TwatBook @KillHershey
Instagram: @Tweet4TwatBook @KillHershey
Facebook: Tweet for Twat Book

CONTENTS

ACKNOWLEDGMENTS

I'm going to go with an unconventional method of writing this -- no fillers or additives. I want to make this as short and sweet as possible so, First and foremost, I have to put God first; without Him nothing is possible.

Margarette Sauveur, where do I begin…you have been the driving force behind my aspirations. A strong woman doesn't even begin to describe your character -- selfless, nurturing, compassionate, and understanding. You've endured so much and made so many sacrifices for me and my four siblings. Thank you Mummie…you are the epitome of love.

My brothers and sisters— Mondia, Fred, Berlandgie, and Benjamen— thank you for always putting up with my bossy behind. I don't say this a lot because of my ego issues, but I love you guys! Mondia, I used you as one of my guinea pigs for this project; I want you to know that if I could somehow shelter you and Bergie from the headaches of dating, I would. Big Ben— try not to be too much of a heartbreaker Hun.

Greg A Paul -- you have been there through my ups and downs. We haven't always seen eye-to-eye, but somehow things always balance out. You are a rare human being. If I could take you back to my planet I would, lol. Thank you for always encouraging and bringing out the best in me.

I owe a special thank you to a very close friend of mine and my graphic designer, Mordecai Ray. Thank you for never judging me, Cai— you make my visions come alive.

To my childhood friend- Cathy Pierre— thank you for always supporting me. I am so grateful to still have you in my world.

And lastly, thank you to all my Facebook, Twitter, and Instagram friends and supporters for letting me into your virtual lives and allowing me to share some of your words. Bisou!

Disclaimer

I know you are used to picking up relationship books and flipping the cover open, and the introduction starts off with something similar to this: This book will teach you the secrets to catching and keeping a man…This book will help you increase your chances of finding a soul mate…This book will give you super-powers and blah, blah, blah.

Well, this book is not going to give you super-powers! I am not a magician, psychic, nor am I a psychologist. I'm just a real woman from the real world with real life experiences. This all began with a letter I started writing the last guy I was seeing. You know that type of letter you write with no intentions of actually sending it to the actual person it was intended for— so in reality I was essentially writing this letter to myself. I needed a way to put things in perspective, so I started writing about my disapproval of the modern-day dating tango, and this somehow became one of the longest letters I have ever written. One page led to another, segments came after segments and poof! A book appeared…but like I mentioned before, I have no super powers -- a lot of the topics I touch on are somewhat common sense, but as common as common sense is, some of us fail to use it. There are topics I touch on that a lot of authors shy away from. The flow of this book is a little different than what you are accustomed to because it is written in segments as opposed to chapters. Some subjects I touch on lightly— and others are more in depth. While some of you may share my perceptions on a lot of these topics, I understand a lot of people will find my views and wordings offensive, but I am completely prepared for and open to the criticism.

This book, just like my last relationship, has been an on-again, off-again project. I never thought I could pull so much material from my personal life and from the lives of the people around me. The more I wrote, the more of an epiphany I had. I consider the last person I was seeing my muse -- he was also that one person that made me act out of character -- my eye opener. Before him, I never cared or worried about what the relationship world was like -- I was in my own world really; oblivious to the detriment caused by pop culture and technology. Going through all the challenges and documenting these ups and downs has helped me to grow and pinpoint exactly what I want and don't want in a life partner.

So here's an in-your-face, no-holds-barred perspective of the New Age, dating world and how social networks and the media impact us romantically. While I may not have a PhD or a television show like Dr. Phil, I do hope that my mistakes, methods, trials and observations will help someone grow from their current situation or even inspire someone to go back to the basics.

This book is inspired by actual events. Some of the characters, incidents, storylines, have been altered or modified for one reason or another. Also, keep in mind that most of these viewpoints are my own.

Enter

INTRODUCTION
VENTING

I'm one of those women that's not accustomed to the modern dating game; all of my relationships have been long-term. When I'm fresh out of a relationship and people ask me how or why I'm single, I facetiously tell them I just did two consecutive 9 and 5 year bids, so I put myself on probation for now. I was always afraid of committing completely to someone, yet I managed to be in long-term relationships. Makes no sense I know, but when I finally got into my first real relationship, I was lucky enough to find someone who understood my fear. Every few months or so when I felt things were getting too heavy, I would tell him exactly how I felt, and he would fall back a bit until my feelings of suffocation subsided. Although we had a lot of issues between the two of us, one of the things that kept us together for as long as we were, was our willingness to communicate -- well maybe it was just my willingness to communicate and his great acting skills and powerful manipulation tactics.

I used to give Lance (the 9 year bid guy -- my first everything) what I refer to as an infidelity detox -- at the end of each year I would have a sit down with him, in an effort to clear the air and lay everything out on the table -- I felt there was no need to carry the past bullshit into the new year. I told him, "listen...this is your opportunity to tell me anything and everything you feel may hurt me in the future. Everything you tell me now you'll get a pass on -- I won't even use it as a reference or as a leverage card in the future...but if I find out anything on my own, and you already know I have the capabilities to do so -- I'm simply leaving you. Know that as a woman, if I ask you a particular question pertaining to an incident...chances are— I already know the truth. I just want to see if you'll lie to me or how far you're willing to carry this lie."

I did this because (1) I firmly believe if you're woman enough to ask a question, you have to be woman enough to accept the truth and deal with the circumstances and consequences of said truth; and (2) When shit rises to the surface, it gives you the opportunity to evolve, let go, and move on -- whether it's moving on from that specific situation or your significant other. A yearly cleansing is beneficial to a healthy relationship. Well, only if you're one of those people that can handle the truth.

Anyhow, Lance was a known pathological liar, so this method didn't work with him as it should have. He was never man enough to lay it all out. He would tell me about a few infidelities, most commonly the lesser offenses, which I had no choice but to get over because I gave him my word that I would -- and like they say, "A man will be a man." I had personal flaws of my own, and I somehow thought his actions were a form of tit-for-tat. He claimed some of his infidelities where due to the fact that I wasn't affectionate enough or that I didn't make him feel wanted or attractive anymore. He also complained that the relationships I have with my male friends made him a bit jealous at times. I'll admit -- I am a little more in touch with my masculine side and sometimes lack in the emotional department, but this was never intentional. I often hear these same complaints from the women around me, so when I heard it from a man, I saw it as sign of sincerity rather than a form of manipulation -- or just tired-ass excuses. Silly me! We women often find ways to justify the means of staying in a fucked up relationship; we see undertones or more often the full-color spectrum before we see the plain black and white picture. We worry more about losing that person instead of trying not to lose ourselves.

The day I took my power back: Lance always had a habit of buying sunflowers and coincidentally, I would always have bad dreams of him committing a cardinal sin prior to me receiving flowers. Most women have intuition, I have dreams. One morning I woke up feeling uneasy -- it was raining cats and dogs outside and all kinds of thoughts were running through my head. I picked up my phone to call him and question him about his whereabouts, but I had a change of heart and rested the phone back down. Right before the phone hit my bed, it rang -- it was Lance calling, I took this as a sign. I answered the phone, and immediately he started going on about how he misses me and wanted to know if I received the flowers he sent me that morning. I stopped him in the middle of his chatter and simply replied, "I don't want to do this anymore Lance...I don't enjoy this feeling or these dreams -- I want out, it's over...I need my peace of mind." This left him confused -- and for the first time he finally laid everything out on the table and confessed the truth entirely. By then it was too late— I chose ME…my peace of mind was more important to me than a relationship title.

I wouldn't consider myself a conventional woman. I was never one of those girls that grew up with the thoughts of getting married, having 2 plus kids and living happily ever after -- although most of the men I've encountered have been conventional men and made attempts to lock me down with the whole marriage and kids thing. Finding the perfect mate was the last thing on my mind— but usually what happens when you are not really looking for something serious is that something serious finds you…

After coming out of a 9 year on-again off-again relationship with Lance, I decided to start dating myself. I figured it would help me grow and would enable me to pinpoint exactly what I want from the opposite sex. So I got into a relationship with Claudia… This meant traveling alone, eating alone, movies alone, and of course…lots and lots of internet porn and having sex…alone.

SIDEBAR: You may want to hold off on the early judgments because believe me; I will be saying far more appalling things throughout this book -- so brace yourself. **You've been warned!

Anyhow after months of…well a year and five months of "making love to myself," I remember receiving a friend request via myspace.com a place for friends from a very handsome gentleman…We'll call him… "Mr. BLACK" for now. He had a very familiar face, but after going through so much in my previous relationship, I didn't bother to even look through his online photos. We chatted for weeks online, mainly about my last breakup and what I was going through…I'm a Gemini, so I lose interest very, very quickly, and oddly enough, he kept me entertained and kept my attention…so I took the next step and checked out the rest of his online photos. I remember ***L***aughing ***O***ut ***L***oud when I realized who he was. The amusing part is I had a flashback of being in front of Club Opium (South Beach, Miami) with my younger sister, Mondia and my girlfriend, Sonia. We were meeting some guys out there, and the guy I was "assigned to" introduced me to Mr. Black…I leaned over and whispered into Sonia's ears, "I want him," she giggled and whispered, "What do you want me to do? And what about him?" referring to the guy I originally came out to meet. "Don't worry…I'm gonna get him." I replied. We both giggled…ahhh to be young, dumb and full of cum.

Five years later, Mr. Black finds me on said social network… I found this ironic! So now that I figured out who he was, I played it cool and gave him my number…I told him my eyes where killing me from staring at the computer screen and that he should call or text me.

After a few weeks of texting, we decided to meet up…Our "second" first encounter was at club Cameo on South Beach…I brought my sister Mondia and my home-girl Tashell. He brought two friends that were visiting him from Bermuda. Being in the same room with him felt intoxicating. This had to be more than just chemistry because I've never been more turned on by just the presence of a man. The word *horny* could not describe what I was feeling, but still I played it cool…"self-control," I told myself.

Some time passed…

"The *Big*.com"

I remember telling myself, "Claudia you're a grown-ass woman! You like him…so why not? Sitting in Mr. Black's living room, I was downing a special mixed drink he called ummm "Tia Breeze"-- if I remember correctly. I tend to over think things, and I live in my head -- so I sat there in his living room, going back and forth with my alter egos in my head (I have four by the way, lol). Where was I? Oh yeah, I'm going back and forth about which one of my alter egos should come out and play. Tipsy and still sipping on what I renamed "Courage in a Cup," I hear him whisper, "Come here." I turn to find his tall, dark and handsome ass standing in the doorway of his room; I play like a big girl and follow him in.

Robin Thicke is playing in the background, and Mr. Black pulls me on to the bed next to him. I'm nervous…so I ask him for another drink. He leaves the room, and minutes later he re-enters with a drink in his hand -- I take it to the head and breathe in deeply as he places his left hand on my thigh. I become anxious and weak all at the same time, and my body begins to quiver…This felt like I was losing my virginity all over again -- he gently takes my hands and tells me to, "Relax, we don't have to do this if you…" I stopped him mid-sentence and replied, "No, I want this."

He leaned in and tried to remove my clothes, I pulled away and told him I would do it myself as I quickly hopped up from the bed and non-seductively removed my t-shirt and jeans. As my jeans hit the floor, I jumped right under the covers. Still shaking, the foreplay began…

"Mmmmmm How old are you again?" I remember asking him, "Twenty-five" he replied. "This doesn't feel like Twenty-five," I giggle -- He enters me…I pull back in an attempt to slide away, he pulls me closer to him. Nervously, I look him in the eyes and whisper "Okay…I'm ready."

Soft key strokes before he logs on to my dot com…I close my

eyes as he gives me his hard drive… pain… megabytes… I pull away. More key strokes…he re-enters me…I close my eyes as I try to come to terms with what was inside of me. Heart racing, body squirming…sweet pain…he uploads…I download…I'm hooked.

Shift

IT'S A SMALL WORLD AFTER ALL

"It's a world of laughter, it's a world of tears.
It's a world of hopes and a world of fears.
There's so much that we share, that it's time we're aware.
It's a small world after all"

Robert B. Sherman and Richard M. Sherman were right on the money when they wrote Disney's IT'S A SMALL WORLD over two decades ago, and thanks to Tom Anderson (Founder of myspace.com a place for friends), Mark Zukerberg (Founder of facebook), Kevin Systrom and Mike Krieger (Founders of Instagram), it's an even smaller world. These founders established a way to capitalize on our obsession with the internet and technology. Whether you admit it or not, everyone has a bit of voyeurism within. This is why social networks and the media are so big. We get a first-hand look into the lives of friends, family, colleagues and even celebrities, without the guilt of being a pervert or a stalker. There's nothing you can't do or find online, from background checks to online porn and sex, from ordering escorts and mail order brides to ordering pizza and Chinese food for delivery. Everything you need is right at your fingertips and just a click away.

Every time one of these social networks fall off, another one springs up and replaces it, adding more options and ways to intertwine the real world with the virtual world. First AOL chat rooms, followed by BlackPlanet, then myspace.com a place for friends took it to a whole other level. Just when we thought networking couldn't get any more advanced, facebook and twitter came flying in with digital capes on— adding a more simplified yet innovative spin on the whole concept. Every facet of our lives is influenced by the media, technology and the World Wide Web. There is no way around it; it sounds almost frightening when you think about it. It is now a normality to ask for email addresses and social network handles instead of phone numbers and full names when encountering someone for the first time. In fact, if it wasn't for my social accounts, I would fail to remember that I and a few others coexisted in the same city. Although I have the phone numbers of most of my friends, colleagues, and associates programmed into my phone, I rarely reach out to any of them. Social networks keep us connected and indirectly involved in each other's lives. There are so many other pros to having a social account; it's a good way to stay connected, a great way to kill time and keep up with current events, and an easy way to prescreen a potential boy/girlfriend -- but for every ying, there's a yang.

People often joke about being addicted or obsessed with facebook and twitter, but these social network addictions are real and in some cases very toxic. Wikipedia.org describes an addiction as "a *mood altering* substance or behavior despite adverse dependency." The key words here are "*mood altering;*" anxiety, depression, nervousness, jealousy, inability to focus on work or school, loss of sleep and human social skills -- puts a strain on relationships and marriages. These are just some of the side effects of being addicted to social networks. They might as well put warning labels or disclaimers up on the signup pages.

We join these networks to feel more involved and connected with one another, but this habit-forming digital vortex sometimes leaves us feeling more alone than ever. Our excessive compulsion and obsession with the virtual world has caused us to neglect real human interaction and relationships. It seems as though people are logging into their social accounts in the morning to update their statues before even jumping out of bed and brushing their teeth -- it has become part of most of our daily rituals. We update our twitter and facebook statuses more than we update our partners on our emotional status. If these social networks could be inserted into your vein with a needle, they would be illegal and rehab facilities across the world would be over capacity.

"You can advance technology faster than you can change a person." - Michael Hall

"Facebook is 1) an obsession. 2) a distraction. 3) a tracking device. 4) where drama lives. 5) everybody's diary." Facebook should not be your reality, just a place to feed your fictional thoughts." - Gardy Rosiclair facebook

POWER Sisters: MUSIC and MEDIA

Back in grade school, I was one of the first kids in my school to have my very own personal computer and phone line in my room. One of the methods I used as a flirting tool was sending and receiving e-cards or music clips via email to and from the guy I liked at the moment. I was able to fall deep in "like" with him through R&B song lyrics alone. So much so that one of my ex's used to call my phone, and when I answered he would play a love song and when it ended, he would quickly hang up without saying a word. This always gave me butterflies in my stomach, and I would go on a search to find the perfect song to play back to him when he called again.

Gone are the days when R&B set the tone of some of our relationships. Now it seems as though the new trend is to do as rappers do. This has been going on for a few years, but I thought after a certain age people would stop using rap lyrics to justify their actions. I've actually had a couple people quote rap lyrics when trying to describe their point of view on a subject. Our generation is so absorbed with so much of the superficial and material factors of life that we forget the basics— sadly there are more dramatics than romantics.

Reality TV has the same effect rap music has on this generation. I would love to say that it only has these influences on "young adults," but unfortunately, this is no longer the case. There's power in reality TV, pop culture and the media. Although primarily scripted, reality television is shaping people's concept of (real)ity. Pop icons and television personalities now hold some of the most influential platforms in modern society. These celebrities have the capability to mold thoughts and inspire actions through music, television and now social networks. From self image to what we wear, drink, eat, listen to and experience -- everything is influenced through the media. Alternatively, people now have expectations set by these media outlets -- we are being fed bullshit through a box made of plastic and glass -- and the majority of society is not only eating up the trash -- they are actually trying to live it.

"He's Hip Hop... I'm Rock...Rock beats scissors (Hip Hop), but with a little passion and R&B we'll give birth to twins and name them Jazz and Soul." - @KillHershey

"Music for one, says a lot about the person you're getting to know, their choice of music in particular. I'd imagine if I were dating a woman to where she and I lived together; R&B and Love songs would play daily when we're at home together. I'm a Lover at Heart, and the music will remind us of us. It has a strong influence...I can't overlook this fact. In the past, the music reminded you of why the love existed, why it lasted and why it's good to stay where you're at. – Michael Forbes

GOING BACK TO DIAL-UP
"The BASICS"

Remember when dating someone was as simple as, "I saved you a seat," and finding out how someone felt about you was as easy as passing a note in class that read, "Do You Like Me? Circle YES or NO?" I remember having a locker full of love notes back in grade school. Now it's just a facebook inbox full of uncreative one-liners and dozens of facebook POKES, although I'm still confused about the whole poking concept. A few years back, I dated someone that still had the right idea when it came to courting a woman, but at the time I wasn't mature enough to appreciate his gesture, and I dubbed him crazy. Well in a way he was a bit crazy, but I realize now he only had good intentions. After dating Manny for a short while, he rewrote a popular song at the time for me, three handwritten pages of him expressing himself. That wasn't the crazy part; it was the way he chose to deliver the letter that freaked me out. He somehow got through my guard gate which was like getting through Fort Knox at the time, and he left the letter in my mailbox then called and told me to go downstairs to check the mail. When I asked him how he knew I was home at that very moment, he sheepishly replied, "Trust me, I know." This freaked me out; I took it for some kind of fatal attraction plot.

Recently while going through my storage room, I came across a box full of old love letters and notes. Reading through a few of them had me on cloud nine; it was like going through an emotional time machine. If old words written on plain notebook paper held this much power, why weren't more people going back to the basics? And *why didn't I appreciate these letters and the people that wrote them until now?* As humans we often take things for granted; only when something is missing is it truly appreciated for the good it brought to your life, only then will you see the value. So what has changed from then to now and how do we get that "old thing back?"

You don't often find something or someone worth

appreciating, the key is to recognize it while it's here, living in that moment -- living in the NOW. When you stop focusing on the artificial and superficial context of a relationship, you leave room for the organic components to fall into place.

"Relationships are harder now because conversations became texting, arguments became phone calls, and feelings became status updates." – Unknown twitter

"Relationships last longer when Facebook doesn't know about them" - Phl S Mdra facebook

"Sex has become a part of the norm, so much so that it is not valued as much as it once was. People now have sex just to have sex... because of parties and social networks sex is now devalued. To most people it's just something to do. The sad part of that outlook is that, sex is a spiritual ritual, were two bodies connect and express the passion and sensuality of one another— through body mind and soul. The expression of that art is now being downplayed to fit in with TV and shallow minded individuals that make it seem as though looks and sex is the only things that keeps a relationship flowing." - Vincent Moore facebook

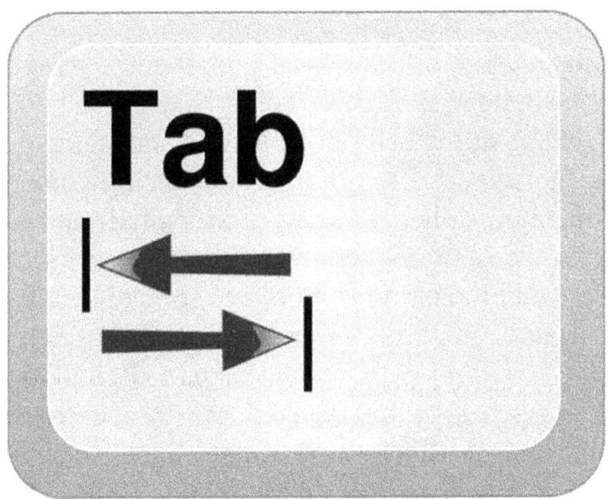
Tab

Lost in TEXT-lation

Technology is both a blessing and a curse; gone are the days when we have to sit by the phone waiting for that special someone to call. We went from saying Hello verbally— to sending out long emotional texts and getting a one word reply in return— or even worse no reply at all.

I remember when Caller ID initially came out and like magic; you could see and were offered the option to ignore who was calling. You no longer had to answer every single call anytime the phone rang in hopes that it was that special someone. Ten years later— I now have a fear of being that person that calls a man and— he stares at his cell phone screen and immediately sends me straight to voicemail. I'm not a fan of leaving voice messages on a man's voicemail either. Leaving a voicemail and not receiving a call back would definitely put a bad taste in my mouth towards that person, so as a precaution I opt out of the voicemail option. To me -- a voicemail is an extra— it means I took that extra step to get in touch with you, and as a result, there's digital footprints left as evidence. Technology has caused me to fear reaching out to a person of interest first—a fear of phone rejection I suppose. Imagine what effect this has on my dating life.

When dating someone new, I feel it is important to point out what you will or won't tolerate from the beginning. I've learned from personal experience if you allow someone to do something in the beginning, the chances of you getting him/her to change are slim to none. I was seeing Mr. Black for over five years, and the biggest problem we had was his obsession with texting. Even on important dates and occasions, he would send a text -- this grinds my gears. When I finally decided to voice my annoyance, he simply said "this is how I am…this is how you met me."

How could I argue with that?

This new way of communicating is killing our ability to carry on real one-on-one conversations. In addition to the lack of real communication— texting and email messages can also be very incriminating when you're involved with someone. One of the things I used to do with all my text messages and emails was save or lock in all the ones I received from my significant other. I kept these messages for months maybe even years, especially if it was a text argument. I did this so that I could revisit a discussion to prove or point out a fact. This eliminated that "I never said this or that" factor. Like every other woman, I used to think I was always right in the event of an altercation. I had the gift of blocking out a man in such a way it almost felt like a super power. Until my most recent involvement with Mr. Black, a man couldn't tell me anything! One of the things I realized was that some of our arguments escalated because of the response time or the lack of a full and complete explanation when it came to text arguments; there was also the factor that I often mistook the tone of a text message or read the message incorrectly. I noticed that when face-to-face during a disagreement, we rarely raised our voices. In fact, we actually sat side-by-side or face-to-face and spoke in a calm tone; I've even held his hand or rubbed his back during some of our disagreements.

Here are some of the issues that arise when texting is the primary basis of communication when dating or in a relationship. I'm listing some easy solutions to help mollify some of the friction texting causes in relationships. I would say stop texting altogether, but I understand that our generation is very dependent on texting and technology, so there's almost no way around it.

Problem: *Constantly checking the phone for new text messages or updating your social network status while on a date.*

Solution A: When on a date, keep your phone in your pocket or handbag. If you need to check your phone because you've been expecting an important text, phone call or email; excuse yourself to the restroom or step outside. *If stepping outside,* be sure to explain yourself so that your actions won't come across as suspicious.

Solution B: If you're at the other end of this texting fiasco;

use a joke to make a point. Say something like "Maybe we should ask the waiter for an extra chair for your phone." Or "The first person to pick up or use their phone pays the bill."

Problem: *Booty Calling aka Butt Dialing*. It has happened to the best of us…dumb things people do with smart phones. Place it in our back pockets, sit on it and it butt dials your significant other. Sometimes this happens while you're in a compromising situation -- or when talking to a friend about something or someone you have no business talking about.

Solution: This is a simple one, are you ready? PUT YOUR PHONE ON LOCK.

Problem: *Sending or receiving abbreviated or acronym short word texts.* Ex. WYD? TTYL, etc. -- I, for one, am not a fan of these abbreviated texts; I have no idea what most of them mean. In my opinion, it comes across as lazy and leaves too much room for misinterpretations.

Solution: Fully write out your messages. Yes, I understand that 160 characters may not be enough to get your point across, but there are other ways around that. Try using different words or if that doesn't solve the problem, send an email or better yet…call the person!

Problem: *Your text question goes unanswered.* Texting is a great tool for *escape artists* -- you send out an emotional text or urgent question to someone, it goes unanswered and that person can easily claim they never received the text when questioned about it later.

Solution: Anything important or emotional should not be said over text messaging. Pick up the phone and call that person. Texting leaves too much room for interpretations, sometimes it's hard for a person to distinguish whether or not you are sad, angry, sarcastic, joking etc. Your feelings and emotions at the time may also influence your interpretation -- the only way to make sure he/she hears where you're coming from and for you to get a prompt response is by calling.

Problem: - *The Impatient Texter.* I am guilty of this one myself; I hate when someone texts me, and I respond immediately only to be kept waiting on a reply.

Solution: Unexpected things happen. Yes that person did text you first, but who knows what may have happened from the time he or she sent out the text to the time you replied; driving, bathroom, clients…things happen, so don't sweat it. If it overly irritates you -- *when the person finally replies*, just nonchalantly point out the wait time. Say something to the effect of: "Hope things are alright with you, I answered your text earlier but didn't know if you got it or not."

Problem: - *Finding a text in his or her phone and reading way too much into it.*

Solution: First off, if you have to look through your significant other's phone, your biggest problem isn't a text. You have trust issues, and *if there's no trust in a relation-ship you might as well abandon "ship" and replace it with "shit".* Now, if it was by accident that you came across this third party text, it's best you don't make any assumptions -- ask before drawing any conclusions.

Problem: *Sending a compromising text to the wrong person.*

Solution: To be frank with you… I have no solution to this text mishap so you're on your own, kiddo! Lol.

Problem: *"Send Me a Picture"* Oh Boy! One of the sure-fire ways to ruin a great text conversation with me is to interrupt with a picture request. If you're just starting to get to know someone and he asks you for a picture -- 9 times out of 10, he is expecting a saucy or risqué one.

Solution: You can (a) send him just a head shot or (b) text back, "I'll send you a pic in due time" or "You'll get a pic if you play your cards right." Note: This puts him on an earning system. Also— always be cautious of who you send your photos to. Remember every phone and email account has a forward function; there is no way of controlling where your photo may end up, so *when in doubt don't send your private parts out.*

Problem: *The Break Up Text--* ***"I can't do this anymore, I'm sorry."***

Solution: The mature and respectful thing to do when ending things with someone is to do it face-to-face or at least with a proper phone conversation -- voice messages don't count. Unless you're in a long distance relationship, there are no justifications or excuses.

Here are a few other texting **DON'Ts**

- Don't try to resolve your conflicts over text messages. If you receive a questionable text, take the time out to call the person and fully hear them out before retaliating.

- Don't send incriminating or hurtful texts. Remember they can be archived. If it sounds like something you wouldn't want to read or hear yourself, don't send it. Put yourself in that person's shoes.

- Don't send out "Helper" texts, or what I like to refer to as *Fire Rescue or Paramedic texts* (Depending on the situation). *"Are you there?" "Why are you not answering?"— "Did you get my message(s)?"*-- Of course he or she got your message(s); they just don't feel the need to send you a reply.

- If you are too much of a coward to say something to someone's face, then don't text it either, no point in being a text bully.

- Take the time to read and edit your text before sending it out. Don't be a victim of auto-correction.

- Don't leave room for interpretation. Express your thoughts clearly.

- Don't substitute texting for genuine one-on-one conversation; use it as a way to stay connected on day-to-day occurrences, not as a primary means of communication.

Examples of sentiments that should not be expressed through text:

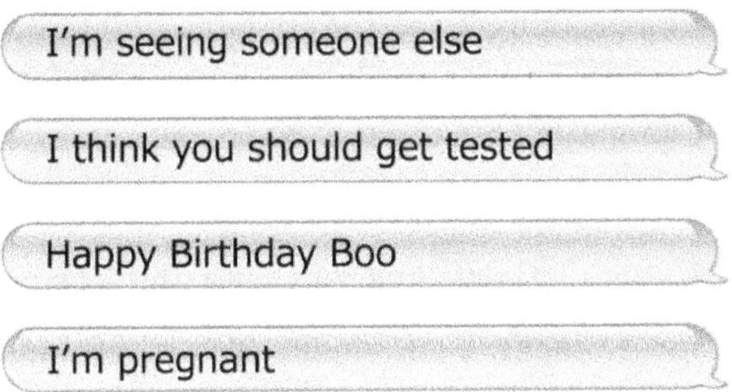

If you need any explanations as to why these texts shouldn't be sent out -- all is lost.

"95% of people text things they could never say in person!" - G-Anthony Moore facebook

Let's Talk About SEX*ting*...

We have graduated from phone sex and moved on to dirty *sexting.*

Sexting - the act of sending out sexual texts or explicit multimedia messages back and forth.

With men being visual creatures and women being so imaginative, it is apparent why this phenomenon is so popular. This new texting epidemic has caused flirting to go from PG13 to rated R with just a click of the send button. Sexting is becoming more and more common with both young and mature adults, but how do you know if the recipient can be trusted with what most might consider incriminating photos and evidence? Everything that is sent out over any device or gadget leaves an electronic trail or footprint; texts, multimedia messages, emails, voicemails, etc. Once you send something personal out into the cyber world, there's no getting it back. I've come across facebook and Instagram accounts dedicated to exposing explicit photos of people— one of the most recent ones I've discovered is "Ex-girlfriends Exposed." The accounts list email addresses to send photos and names of the people you would like to expose. With accounts like this out there, what are some of the safety measures you can take to protect your privacy?

DO's and DON'Ts to SEXting

Speaking from personal experience -- receiving an unexpected explicit photo from someone I just started to get to know is just plain creepy and is not in the least bit stimulating. Both parties have to be *willing participants*.

- TRUST: Make sure you trust the person you are sending your photos to, remember there are always risks when sharing something personal, you must always be cautious.
- When sending racy pictures, try not to show your face and body in the same photo, and try to conceal any tattoos, birthmarks or distinguishing piecing.
- DELETE. ERASE. REMOVE. OBLITERATE all traces of evidence after sexting, and ask the other participant to do the same.

Safe Sexting Is The Best Sexting. There are no condoms or nondisclosure agreements for sexting, so the only way to protect yourself entirely is to not send out photos, try to stick to using *just words.*

BONUS: *Sexting Game*

You Show Me Yours, and I'll Show You Mine

Instructions To Playing The Game: Start off by sending your game partner a head shot photo with the caption "Follow my lead..." -- After receiving a head shot in return, send your partner a photo of your chest area, followed by your mid-section and so on and so on.

Object of The Game: Getting both players to comfortably reveal themselves equally. With both partners evenly exposed, there's less chances any of the players will do anything to incriminate the other, thus creating an equal playing field.

The 7 Deadly Sins of Social Networks

In the early stages of dating, it is critical that you don't become a statistic and let these social networks ruin your chances of building your connection with that special someone of interest. Some of the things I am about to list, I have committed or have fallen victim to.

Social Sin 1. *Following or adding that person as a friend too soon* - I've found that this is where the issues begin. Everyone is different, and so is every relationship and situation, but if either one of you are the jealous type, then it's probably best that you don't add each other on any social network site too early on -- it may cause friction.

*Be sure to tell the person why you don't think it's a good idea to follow or add each other as friends in the beginning -- because some might mistake this preventative measure as disrespect or think that you're ashamed of them.

Social Sin 2a. *Posting certain pictures that would be deemed disapproving to your mate* - Before posting a picture, make sure to ask yourself how would he or she view and feel about this photo? Photos lead to assumptions and conflicts. Common sense may not be common in the social network world, but it is still inexpensive, so please acquire it.

Social Sin 2b. *Posting way too many pictures of yourself and bragging* - Nothing repels more than self-absorption.

Social Sin 3. *Sweating the small stuff; try not to take everything so literally* - Every tweet is not a sub-tweet and most importantly…Every tweet or status update is not about you.

Social Sin 4. *Don't judge an account by its followers* - Having the most followers or likes doesn't mean that person is popular or well connected in the real world, remember quality over quantity.

Social Sin 5. *Marking your territory* - Writing all over your significant other's page, "LIKING" all of their photos or re-tweeting most of his/her tweets just to show up in their mentions is not going to stop another woman from going after him/her, it only makes you look possessive or crazy.

Social Sin 6. *Arguing, venting or airing out your relationship issues on your timelines* - Think of twitter and facebook as a party or restaurant setting. You wouldn't break out into an argument with your partner or air out your dirty laundry in front of hundreds of people right? So why do it on a social network where you both may have friends and followers in common?

Social Sin 7. *Being a serial social lover* - I follow someone on one of my social accounts, and every week this girl is either in love or getting her heart broken. Try to remember people can go on your timelines and read your past updates. It's a turn-off to see updates about different people you dated in such a short span of time; it shows you move way too fast.

Following someone on Twitter is a great way to stop having a crush on them. - @WhitneyCummings twitter

Here is a very good example of what men see and perceive from some women's status updates:

"First you give us every gruesome detail of how he hurt you; one would expect that you are waiting for him, to POP up on your status, and give you a public apology; but he doesn't so your next post is that you are done...still no response from him. A month goes by, and you start flirting with other men on Facebook, announcing that you are ready to date again...still no response from him, so you wait another month and then finally break down

and confess your love for him, contradicting everything thing you said before. Still no response from him... and you will never get a response from him because he knows just how to control a young-minded woman like yourself. He will continue to sleep with you whenever he feels like it because you allow him to. You love the drama, you feed on the pain and even though you're furious and enraged, you repeat that cycle. You update your status with "I Am Done," but you are not done because you are in love...you are in love with a little boy. You don't deserve a real man because all you will do is prevent him from finding a real woman. In the end, you will waste a REAL man's time and leave him to chase after what you love...which is "little boys." - David Manuel facebook

Giving Up the BOX via INBOX

In this day and age where a man or woman can order up a booty call via inbox, what's the point of even dating and getting to know someone? With sex being so easy to attain, people rarely take the time out to get to know each other and build that essential bond or connection. In a generation where women fuck for car keys and men trick instead of treating, what are our options? It has gotten to the point that athletes, celebrities and entertainers are using these sites and networks to pick up women. So, for the ones that still believe in the old-fashioned dating and courting ritual, how can we use the internet and technology to our advantage?

Recently I sat down at a little café with my sister and a male friend. While discussing a number of miscellaneous things, he asked me about what I was writing. I gave him a brief description, and we started to talk about the impact social networks have on modern society and how easy it is for a man to acquire sex through facebook and other social networks -- a lot of men use inbox messages sort of like Batman's bat signal. He went on to tell me how a few of his buddies would, when going out of town, send out facebook and twitter direct messages to 40 or so women in their arrival city announcing they would be coming into town – and as a result, maybe 10 out of these 40 ladies would set up a location and time to link up -- 4-5 out of the 10 ladies would then have sexual relations with these men -- very good odds, might I say.

A man will give you his bank card pin, access to his personal finances, social security number, his last name, and have unprotected sex with you -- but his social network or phone password he protects and keeps secret by any means necessary. Why do you think that is?

facebook and twitter are the ultimate Little Black Book -- a practical way to keep contact with past mates as well as potential dates -- a convenient way to keep tabs on dating, romance, or just sexual escapades. With the protection of a secured password, you can access your online love life from a number of electronic devices. I pointed out before that there are pros and cons to this tech world.

Let's take facebook for example, while there are obvious cons, I think it's great that you can log on to someone's facebook page after meeting him or her and be able to get a feel of what they're into or what's important to them. This is one tool that can be used to predetermine whether or not this is someone you would be interested in getting to know further. This saves you time, an outfit and maybe even some makeup in the event you do have a date option on the table. While social networks can put a strain on some relationships, it *can* be beneficial to others. Take people in long distance relationships for instance— with so many miles in between two lovers, having a means to see each other through social cams or being able to stay updated through pictures and statuses can be helpful to a relationship. Seeing photos of a loved one constantly has similar effects of making eye contact, it helps build an emotional connection. You know how they say, "out of sight, out of mind"...*well, in sight keeps the bond tight.*

FOOL-osophers

It seems as though a lot of people on these social networks think they are modern-day philosophers or a life expert. Through the miracle of cut and paste, someone can cut up bits and pieces of someone else's thoughts, add their own personal bullshit to spice it up and just claim the whole theory as their own. It would seem as though all of these experts are on a righteous path to obscurity. In an attempt to sound deep or profound they give advice on something they know nothing about, using borrowed or should I say stolen words without actually quoting or giving credit to the original writer. Time and time again, I've logged onto my accounts and scrolled down my timeline only to find someone that's not fit to be giving advice going in about this, that and the third. The FOOLish part about it is they don't live by example or even attempt to follow their own counsel. The saying "practice what you preach" comes to mind every time I see one of these Fool-osophical status updates. Stating things just to state them or just to get more "Likes" or "Re-tweets." There's a huge difference between being motivational and just blowing smoke. What makes matters worse is that a lot of people buy into the bullshit. Occasionally, I take the time out to read some of the comments people post in response to a fool-osophical status update. I do this only to see if I'm the only one smelling the BS.

Hoe-losophy

Red Bottom Hoe: *Ruth is a single, self-proclaimed model. She loves the ball players and entertainers and they "love" her, too. Purses, shoes, trips, she gets them all and will "do it all" to get them. She takes to her social networks to post half-naked pictures and to call out other females she dubs as "haters," then attempts to give advice on how to keep a man.*

Man-Hoe: *Justin has thousands of female followers from around the world and a good amount of male followers as well. Justin's updates are mainly about how a man should be loyal to one woman, how to treat a lady and how much of a good man and gentlemen he is -- he gets hundreds of likes and re-tweets daily* *and his women followers dream of being with a man like Justin. Justin's job allows him to travel around the US -- so while his main lady waits at home for him, Justin sets up "tweet & greets" with some of his followers and shows them firsthand what it's like to "experience" a man "like him."*

Hoe in Sheep's Clothing: *Raquel is a law school graduate turned party/event planner, lives in the city, has a job she loves, friends she adores and is pursuing a man that is currently attached to another woman. Raquel also has a reputation for doing what most would refer to as hoe-ish activates with more than one man at the same time…on camera. Yet on her social network accounts, she quotes Bible verses and makes references to other women's bad deeds. Her social accounts give her the platform to portray herself as righteous and upright.*

The Reformed Hoe: *Judith has a similar past to Raquel's. The only difference is she is now married with children and feels her marriage certificate erases her past reputation and validates her. Subliminal emotional rants on her Facebook page is her specialty. She tries to generalize her statements by using the words "people" or "someone" when it's apparent the status update is specifically tailored for her significant other.*

More commonly these days' first impressions are made from viewing someone's social account. With Photoshop and lies, a person can make you believe whatever they want you to believe. I'm sure you or someone you know has been intrigued by someone they met online but was totally disappointed when meeting that someone in person. There are a lot of pros and cons to the social world -- while most people lie about their lives online; it's refreshing to know that social networks can be a great tool to reveal some of these lies. From misleading profile pictures to people tweeting and updating their statuses about popping bottles and stating that their lives are movies, but in actuality their lives are really low budget (real)ity "shows" -- everything is scripted and rented -- even down to their personalities and character. In reality their facebook and twitter statuses are doing more living then they actually are -- you just have to learn to read between the ***lies.***

Tales from the book... facebook

MEET AND FREAKS

Cheating doesn't only affect the person that's being cheated on; it can sometimes affect the person doing the act. Edwin met a woman on facebook and started having sexual relations with her. One day while in the middle of doing "the act," the woman he was cheating with answered her cell phone and had a full on conversation with her boyfriend while Edwin was still inside of her. Although he concluded "the act," the whole ordeal freaked him out. He started thinking maybe his lady is capable of doing the same thing. Edwin's relationship went downhill from there; his mind started playing tricks on him, every time he called his lady he couldn't help but to get flashbacks. His cheating habits were coming back to haunt him. Edwin started projecting his guilt, and these projections manifested into insecurities. He started questioning his lady's whereabouts and who she was communicating with on her social network accounts. As a result of Edwin's online sexual meet and freaks, his relationship got declined and blocked.

IN A RELATIONSHIP WITH...

After too many months of dating, Dion's suitor finally worked up the courage to ask her to be his girlfriend. Now Dion wants to change her facebook relationship status to "In A Relationship *with*.... "When is it a good time to change my facebook status to "In A Relationship *with...*" she asked. My answer:

"Me personally, I'm a private person when it comes to relationships. I don't like posting who I'm in a relationship *with* because it only invites drama and somehow gives off the sense that you're marking your territory. If you're one of the ones that want to profess your love to the world, I think its best you talk it over with your significant other first, so it doesn't come as a surprise when he logs on to his page and sees you added him to your relationship status. You want to be on the same page when it comes to something of this nature. If you don't feel you have to ask him for his permission, saying it in passing is a great way to feel out where his head's at."

You may want to wait at least a month or two before letting the world into your relationship. This will give you guys time to build a concrete foundation; you want to be able to withstand the social network relationship storm— these online networks are distracting and may cause an interference. Also, just in case your relationship is short lived, waiting to change your relationship status will eliminate the frequent "In a relationship"..."Single"..."In a relationship"...again, updates your friends and colleagues have to endure seeing on their social network timelines.

Seems crazy that we now have to second guess or question someone else on whether or not you can claim the person you are involved with publicly, when online dating rules were null and void not too long ago.

Don't Judge a Book by its Cover

You often hear *Don't judge a book (person) by its cover*, well it's a good thing that you can now purchase eBooks online for a fraction of what it would cost to get a paperback; this way you won't feel so cheated if it turns out to be a bad read. There's even an option to sample the first few chapters for free in most cases. It's unfortunate we can't do the same thing with human interactions; I would love to be able to sample before purchasing -- because quite honestly there are some editions I wouldn't add to my library if I were given the option to…at this point I would even settle for a book review.

With all that said… It's safe to say you shouldn't judge a person by their online photos. Going on a date with someone you met online is like going on a blind-date because eight out of ten times there's a huge chance that person will look nothing like their online pictures thanks to filters and Photoshop. While we're on the subject of Photoshop, it seems as though people are using Photoshop to alter much more then profile pictures, they are Photoshopping their relationships and lives, making things appear a lot more alluring than it actually is. If your relationship looks better in pictures than it does in real life, it's time for you to go back into the black room, edit or re-develop something worth photographing and if that fails, just crop your significant other entirely out of the picture.

"I've never understood the person who would rather have public adoration and private failures. Not happy in a relationship, and post pictures projecting happiness. Then wonder why no one is there to help pull them up. It's because no one knows you're drowning." – Jullian Goodin facebook

TALES FROM THE TECH-SIDE

Back in the 90's, there was a television show that came on late at night called *Tales from the Darkside*. It was a science fiction series that depicted strange tales or horror stories that always ended with a twist. With technology being our number one source of communication, it's fair to say we all have a technology-related relationship horror story— I'll start off with a tech infidelity of my own…

After getting out of a long committed relationship with Lance, we went through what I like to call TAP (transitional adjustment period) -- that brief period where you're dating other people but not quite ready to have sex with someone new, so you occasionally allow your ex to "tap" that ass during your brief transition phase. Anyhow, my ex, who was seeing someone new at the time, stopped by to help me "scratch an itch," —before doing the do, he went into the restroom but left his phone behind. Now, I've never been the snooping type, but something took over me… I picked up his mobile device and to my surprise it was unlocked, and by "fate" a text from the new woman popped up on the screen, "What are you up to?" it read. So, right before he stepped out of the restroom I dialed out her number…*now wait just a minute here*! Before you start to judge me…in my defense, she did want to know what he was up to. Continuing from where I left off -- I dialed out her number, and when I heard a voice on the other end say, "Hello," I furtively placed the phone where he left it. I called out his name and seconds later he came out of the restroom. To distract him from picking up his phone and realizing it "dialed out," I quickly started undressing -- all the while saying sexual phrases and adding his name at the end of each phrase— "Tell me how you want it, Lance" -- He played right into it and proceeded to go into full detail of what he wanted me to do to him. After an encore performance, I excused myself and pretended to go freshen up, just to give him enough time to discover what was unfolding. When I came back, he was putting his clothes on in a haste; I giggled inside while he gave me a lame-ass excuse on why he had to leave so abruptly. The moral of the story is…phones can be used as weapons of new-lationship destruction.

iTrack

A male buddy of mine (let's call him Allen) decided to go to a gentlemen's club to have a few drinks with a couple of his lady friends. While at the bar, he received a phone call from his wife; he always made it a point to answer her phone calls -- a sincere effort to prevent any friction between the two of them. After hearing loud music in the background, she asked him of his whereabouts, and he half-truthfully replied, "I'm at a bar, having a few drinks with some potential clients." When she continued to ask him questions, it unnerved him and in an attempt to sound above suspicion, he started to play the victim by heatedly asking her, "What's wrong with you? I said I was with clients…what's the problem?" She replied, "You sure you're not in a strip club? Someone said they just saw you there." He tried to assure her he was just at a bar -- although it was just innocent drinking and his wife was okay with him going to strip clubs from time to time, Allen held his ground and stuck with his lie— guess he figured there was no turning back now. After what he thought was a close call, Allen went back to his office with his friends…he met up with some actual clients that night and then dropped off his companions before heading home.

When he arrived at his house, he was greeted by his furious wife in their driveway. She asked him once again "Where were you?" and still, Allen held his ground. Allen's wife calmly opened up his car door, reached into the back seat, pulled out her iPad, and went on to show him every location he went to for the entire day -- precise address, arrival time and duration of each of his stops. So it turned out, that the "someone" that supposedly spotted him at the strip club was an actual electronic gadget, Allen couldn't even fight his case and therefore entered a guilty plea. Days later when discussing this with me, he said, "She called me today and told me that she still has 79% battery charge left on her iPad…she didn't even charge it up after the incident…which means she could've left that damn thing in my car for a week to track me…I'm so traumatized!" -- My reply, "You got to give it up to her…that was very creative; women make the best detectives."

I gave her an A+ for resourcefulness and creativity.

The Illusionist

Carrie has been in a committed relationship with Kevin for three years, no major issues, but somewhere on the relationship trail Carrie fell off track and started seeing another man on the side. As devoted as Kevin was to Carrie -- Carrie couldn't help but think something was missing. She needed to feel more -- she would attempt to start arguments with Kevin just to see if she could get him to act out of character -- but Kevin would always find ways to diffuse things. To her, things were just too perfect -- so she sought elsewhere for something more intensifying and fervent. A few months went by and to Carrie's surprise; the excitement of dating another man on the side still hadn't worn off. She had the comfort of having a good man at home and the thrill of exploring the unfamiliar on the side.

Some time passed, and Carrie started receiving disturbing text messages from what she assumed was her side diversion's main girlfriend -- unfazed, Carrie continued to carry out her infidelities. Days passed and the disturbing text messages kept rolling in -- the more she received the more details this person would disclose about Carrie's personal life. Seeking out advice, she asked her older sister what to do about the situation. When told to end the affair, Carrie refused -- she enjoyed having her cake and eating it too. After a couple weeks, the texts stopped coming in -- she was relieved that the person finally let up. In the days to come, Carrie started becoming more careless with her actions -- no longer making any attempts to cover her tracks. Her cake dreams were short lived when she discovered her phone had been blocked from making or receiving any calls to her side piece. She failed to remember that when you are on a shared cell phone plan with your mate, you're not only sharing your minutes -- your phone log is also accessible. You see -- Kevin was the person sending Carrie all those disturbing text messages -- he found out early on that Carrie was stepping out on him – one-on-one confrontations are not in his character so he chose a more sneaky, dramatic and not to mention -- just plain out creepy way to get his message across. When that failed, he called the cell phone company and blocked the number— they broke up soon after.

"Confession: Yes, I have cheated on a woman before, but it was never ongoing. I just hit it two or three times and kept it moving, because cheating is too stressful and too much work. You have to erase the text messages before you get home, save the other chic's number under your homeboy's name. You have to make up excuses to sneak off with the other woman and make sure you take her somewhere your girl doesn't frequent or her nosey ass home-girls -- because with the invention of camera phones, they will snap a picture of your ass. You used to be able to say it wasn't you but those days are gone." - David Manuel facebook

Tweet For Twat

Social online dating has become the new norm. While this is a convenient and easy concept when it comes to the new age dating game, most commonly it has a short expiration date. With everyone on the net pretending to be someone they're not, how can you weed out the real from the fake? Is it safe to compare the inter-"net" with a fishing net? Take Tony for instance -- You see, Tony uses social networks like facebook, twitter and TAGGED as his hunting ground *(cue JAWS theme song).* He posts photos of his luxury cars, his lavish trips, lies about his age, hobbies, etc., and women fall for it. When a woman takes the bait, he starts selling them a dream. Unlike other men that just look at a woman's online pictures and comment on their beauty, Tony reads and studies each online bio and picks out specific key words, phrases and interests cited in their bio to capture his prey. He then plants a seed; he tells his prey that he's planning a lavish trip out of state and would love to "maybe" have a special lady accompany him. As obvious and pathetic as this sounds— some women fall for it.

On date one, he makes it casual. He invites her on a group outing and suggests that she invite a friend or two. He does this to (a) make her comfortable and (b) try to win her friends over. Soon he'll have her lady friends doing his dirty work for him. Tony makes sure he shows them a good time and as an unknowing exchange, his prey is bombarded with praises of Tony from her girl friends. His demeanor, clothes, jewelry, car, the amount of cash he pulls out and how much he spends on that first date -- they make a checklist of it all. These tactics break down any inhibitions his prey may have. By date two; their first one-on-one date, Tony's prey is ripe for the taking and he pounces at any indication of weakness. Tony takes full advantage of his prey with no real intentions to follow through with any foregoing promises. By the time his prey finds out she's been set up for the bait and switch, Tony has sailed off in search of a bigger catch.

"The bait always dies."- @KillHershey 

"PlentyOfFish.com is just for what it sounds like, catching fish. I myself enjoy catching and releasing, lol." - @Cashflow23
Instagram

BIG City Dating

I live in what's considered a big city; "slow money, fast pussy" is how I like to describe it. Miami is where the men have champagne dreams on beer bottle budgets and the women sell their twat and soul for a pair of red-bottoms. Living in a city where it's 5 women to every man makes it a challenge to weed out the good from the bad. One of my girlfriends complained about a man who asked her out on a date, and when she asked him what he had in mind, he had the audacity to say, "Why don't you rent a movie from RED BOX and come over to my place?" -- This was his idea of a good first date. Later that month at a dinner party I attended -- the topic of the night was— *Dating in Miami*. One of the men there asked the women "What exactly do women look for in a man, really?" He went on to say that women are confusing because they claim they want a good man, but all he's been witnessing in Miami and other big cities is women chasing after the ball players and entertainers.

My simple response to him was, "Those are the women that haven't quite found themselves yet, they don't know what they want…better yet, need from a man."

My girlfriend Salli's response to him was, "Well we can say the same things about you men. You're attracted to those types of women, that's why you noticed and noted what type of men they're interested in and what they're chasing after." The night went on and one of my male friends, Wayne stated, "I feel sorry for you ladies." When asked, "Why?" He stated "All three of you are smart and very attractive. I'm from Alabama, and down in Alabama, you three ladies would have been married right out of high school because we country boys know when to lock a good thing down, but in a city like Miami these men don't appreciate you. Let's be honest…beautiful women come a dime a dozen down here, so why lock one of you ladies down when a man can have 5 or 6 of you?" —Good question.

Why lock one down when a man can have 5 or 6 women?

I asked this same question to some of the men I know through my twitter, facebook and text messages, and here's a few of the responses I got.

"Juggling is expensive." - @AntonioBarnes twitter

"Stability and Kids" - Tony Grams

"It gets old, and 9 times out of 10 the girl we end up with isn't from a big city." - Leighton Morrison facebook

"A dude gets tired of running the streets, at least good dudes do." - Wayne Anderson - @2Waynes twitter

"Men don't want to be in a relationship when everyone is giving the milk up for free." - Stan Vic facebook

"It takes a balanced person to find a balanced partner. Like the ying and yang, two can't be one circle unless they each know who they are in that circle. In a game of poker, you may win and have fun with a few face cards, but the game gets old without the full deck! I would want to be in a relationship for the long haul, to grow, share, make the journey to the future and be able to look back on the past and remember the one that took the whole journey with me through the ups and downs. No disrespect but those that were ins & outs are getting forgotten."- Seneca Ho Ken facebook

"Why buy the cow when you can get the entire farm for free?"

I want to point out how straight to the point the first few guys were with their response, with men you almost always have to take what they say at face value. I want to close out this section with one of my favorite responses to the questions.

"Well, when we become men and evolve past our man parts, we become picky. When our gratification in life is attached to our man parts, of course a place with a lot of women will always be a party. But when we find our purpose in life, and something to be passionate about, we tend to look for situations and environments that will protect our work in life. The drama of juggling multiple women and the uncertainty of relationships are no longer conducive to our ultimate goal. This is where the line between Men and the "Un-evolved" Male is drawn (Has nothing to do with age). When we begin to represent ourselves as more than just our dicks, we start to look for stability and accomplishment in life, including our women. That's why it is important for women to be prepared as well. As a man evolves, so do his standards for his environment, family and women. The days of women getting by off of exploiting themselves, showcasing sexy outfits, and revealing Facebook *pictures are over when it comes to attracting great men and fathers. As women begin to want that stability, honesty, and certainty in a relationship with men, they begin to feel that saturated environment that they are trying to be recognized in. If you want different, you have to be different." - Coach Lex Kelly of Stand Up Men, Inc.* facebook

He said a mouthful, a lot of non-saturated food for thought.

Date in your BRACKET

Last year while speaking to a male friend, Todd about dating, I expressed how afraid of jumping back into the dating scene I was. I'm accustomed to long-term relationships, and when I'm with someone, I'm fully committed. I tried the Miami dating scene, and it felt like I was on *Hell Date* -- I actually expected a camera crew to hop out a time or two. I went on to list three different scenarios…

HELL DATE SCENARIO 1: *Mr. We Can Do Whatever You Like*

I met *Guy 1* at a club on South Beach, and when he asked me for my number, I gave him my usual line "If I see you around 2 more times, I'll give you my number." Corny line right? Let me explain why I do this…Miami is a big city; although it's big, it constantly reminds you of how much of a small world we live in. Everybody knows everybody -- you've heard of 6 degrees of separation? Well let's just say, Miami has 2 degrees of separation. So whenever I encounter a man I'm attracted to, I use that line in an effort to create enough time for me to do my proper research on him.

Let's get back to my encounter with *Guy 1* -- some time passed and as I predicted, I ran into *Guy 1* on a different occasion. On our second encounter, we had a nice conversation, and he somehow convinced me to exchange numbers with him before our third run in. He also talked me into going on a date with him the next day. I told him I had a meeting with a client in the morning but after the meeting, I was free to link up with him, so *I would give him a call.*

The next morning midway through my meeting, my phone rings. I send it to voicemail and reply with a text that read, "Still in a meeting. I will call you back soon." 30 minutes later, he calls back again and I send it to voicemail… yet again. A text comes in soon after: "You said you would call back SOON." STRIKE ONE!!!!!!

After my meeting, I call him back and ask him where he would like to meet up…He informs me that he recently moved to Miami about a month ago and has no car as of yet but went on to tell me that he would like to sightsee outside of South Beach, so "we could do whatever you like" he says…Long story short, I picked *Guy 1* up, hop on I-95 North and 10 minutes into the drive, he tells me that he only has $40.

PAUSE

I quickly jump off the highway, and head back south to the beach. I didn't want to be a bitch about the situation, so I parked the truck and told him we should go get a slice of pizza. On the way to the pizza shop, *Guy 1* stopped at two stores and tried on a few pairs of shoes, followed by him calling me "Baby," (I hate when a man automatically starts calling me baby prematurely. This tells me he calls every woman he speaks to baby; I don't know about the rest of them, but I like to earn my titles). Anyhow, after the unearned name episode, we ended up at a pizza shop. In an effort to start up a conversation, I asked him to tell me a little about himself. He went on to tell me he has three kids by three different women …STRIKE TWO! He then tells me that his brother -- the one I met the same night I met him -- had a great career, car, house and a bigger "Johnson"…when hearing this I half-jokingly said, "Oh boy, looks like I chose the wrong brother, huh?" -- and as if all that wasn't bad enough, he added the fact that he just did 7 years in jail…STRIKKKKKKKKKKKE THREE! …and that…wait, I don't even think it's worth continuing on with this scenario. I only remember thinking, "Where's Ashton Kutcher when you need him!"

HELL DATE SCENARIO 2: *Mr. I Always Get What I Want*

While at work one fine and sunny day, lol….a co-worker pulls me from my office and tells me a client of his is interested in getting some interior design work done and would like to meet me. His client turns out to be an ex-professional athlete; we chat about the work he would like done and go over a few samples, materials and ideas. At 3:16 p.m. we end our consultation, and he invites me to dinner, I kindly decline and tell him I don't date clients or athletes, and I walk away as quickly as possible. At 4:55 p.m. guess who's still sitting there waiting…sigh. I turn back to head into my office and he calls out, "I'm going to continue to sit here until you agree to go to dinner with me." 6:01 p.m. rolls around. While getting ready to leave work for the day, I hear his voice again, "I always get what I want…you don't want me to start sending obnoxious amounts of flowers and popping up here every other day do you?…just say yes to dinner, I promise you won't regret it.

FAST FORWARD

Hell Date 2 with *Guy 2* is actually going surprisingly well. Good conversation, great choice of restaurant followed by us meeting his friend and his friend's lady for some drinks and dancing. After a couple drinks in his system, he starts to go on and on about his accomplishments. I believe his exact words were "I'm an Ivy League man…didn't your mother ever tell you to marry an ex-ball player with 3 degrees, 2 houses and 4 cars."

SIDENOTE: I couldn't make this stuff up even if I tried.

Continuing on from where I left off -- His friends' girlfriend saves me by pulling me on to the dance floor with her. After a bit of dancing I stop to just enjoy the ambiance -- live band playing, drinks flowing through our systems. A tall gentleman walks up to me and says, "I hope I'm not being rude but I just wanted to compliment you on your beauty." I smile…blink and half way through saying thank you, my date tackles the man into a wall. I'm so embarrassed that I walk out of the bar. This is exactly why I don't date athletes— they have way too much ego. 0_o

HELL DATE SCENARIO 3: *Sergeant Insecure*

After *Hell Date* 1 and 2, I had very low expectations, but can you blame me? *Guy 3* was an army sergeant; he let me pick the place, so I chose a gun range for starters. Now I'm unsure if he was just being a good sport, but his aim was way off. My shooting percentage was higher than his when scoring our target sheets, so that was an ego boost for me considering the fact he's in the army. After the gun range, we went out to dinner; the conversation was going well until he stated, "I bet even if you wore a plastic bag, men would still get at you." At first, I thought it was a form of flattery until he added, "I wouldn't be able to seriously date anyone that looks like you because I would be afraid that any man could steal you away at any time."

STOP

I stared at him with a blank face as he added on to his insecurities, "I wouldn't even feel comfortable with you going outside to get the mail. Every man wants to have sex with a woman that looks like you, but not many of us are confident enough to wife you." Not sure if it was the alcohol during dinner that got him to open up so quickly, but I thanked him for his honesty and called it a night.

After sharing these scenarios with Todd he asked me, "Are you dating in your bracket?" I asked him to elaborate on what he meant and the example he gave me was this, **"The Star Football Player and the Head Cheerleader."** Although he knows I refuse to entertain any advances, from any more athletes or men in the entertainment industry, he tried to convince me that maybe I should give these types of men a second chance. He went on to say that trying to date regular men is probably the reason I still can't find the right fit; these men don't fall in my compatibility bracket. The Cheer Captain dates the Star Athlete because they are of similar ranks and face the same obstacles. Yes opposites do attract as with magnets, but keep in mind that the very little things these two opposites have in common (e.g. race, backgrounds, culture, etc.) is what keeps them connected, and in atypical cases, these small similarities can also pull them apart. So in cases like yours, it's probably best to just scratch out the opposites attract notion and just stick with the "two sides of the same coin" concept -- this means there are diverse but very common features between the two subjects; in this case -- individuals.

Let's go back to your date scenario with *Guy 3* -- he pointed out that while he desires you, he is not equipped to sustain a real relationship with you because of his fear of another man stealing you away -- meaning you are too much of an opposite, so the attraction would lead to self-doubt. This tells me that he was dating way out of his league and bracket. Now, the ex athlete in scenario 2 is confident enough to date you, but his only fault was his ego. Seeing how he went out of his way to court you, I'm willing to bet if you respectfully called him out on his ego, he would make an effort to check it at the door next time."

*Todd made a very good point, and I partially agree with him -- the reason for only partially agreeing is this: The **"Beauty and the Nerd"** equation.*

I've been observing a lot of my friends' relationships over the years, and had a lot of women tell me that they would rather date men that are less attractive because they feel that less attractive men treat women...***correction***...less attractive men treat "beautiful" women like queens, especially in a big city where beautiful women are a dime a dozen. Attractive men are accustomed to encountering women in "their league" that throw themselves at them, so getting laid is effortless. This somehow desensitizes them; they become less appreciative of beauty, and treat these women as objects, play things, or just another option. Now the nerds, and/or should I say the less attractive males, on the other hand, are the ones that went through junior high and high school fantasizing about Ms. Beauty. They go on to college and work their ass off to get that degree -- that will eventually allow them to make the money, that will earn them the power, respect and confidence to get Beauty's attention. This equation works best because Mr. Nerd is accustomed to working hard to get and keep the things he desires -- so in these cases -- opposites do attract.

So if opposites attract…and, acceptable mutual similarities is a rarity, how do you find that balance? Is it safe to say the similarities of these opposites are what can bring and keep them together?

So to add on to the idiom, "Opposites attract, I would say Opposites attract…when and *if they have enough in common.* This is why dating sites have been so successful -- the numbers don't lie, eHarmony.com's tagline states that "1 in 5 Relationships Start Online." More and more people are joining online dating sites in hopes of finding the right mate, and one of the most commonly used tools are compatibility tests. Compatibility tests are created to establish how romantically compatible you are with a potential partner. The founders of these sites realized that it's not so much of the opposites that attract, but it's ordinarily the qualities and things these opposites have in common. Like minds make for better matches so…*How can you implement a real-life compatibility test when seeking out a life partner?*

When dating, asking the right questions can help you weigh in whether or not your potential mate is the right fit for you. Make a list of questions to ask when on a date. These questions will help you identify early on the different qualities and traits this person possesses. Below is a sample list of questions; add on some of the things you feel are important, and this will enable you to make a final decision.

1. What are you looking for -- dating, committed relationship, just sex?

2. What are some of the things you have to offer a partner?

3. Tell me a little about your friends.

4. What's your belief system like?

5. What is the most random thing you've done?

6. What's your best childhood memory?

7. What's your worst childhood memory?

8. Describe your family upbringing.

9. Where are you now and where would you like to be in the future?

10. What's your worst dating experience?

11. What are some of the things you require from a mate?

12. Name something you can never grow tired of doing.

13. Describe a typical day for you.

14. What's your idea of romance?

15. Name one of your regrets in life.

16. Name one thing you would change about yourself if given the chance.

17. If your life was made into a movie, what genre would it fall under?

The TEST DRIVE

With so many temptations and distractions out there, how do you focus on just one individual long enough to grow actual interest? What are some of the key factors you tend to look for or even overlook when seeking out a mate? I'll be quite frank with you— I find dating to be very draining and exhausting. I just don't have the patience or energy to "learn" someone new, so I came up with methods that help me eliminate candidates. When meeting someone in club-like settings -- first impressions are not everything, especially when alcohol is aiding you with the evaluation. You can't judge a person by the exterior. Yes, looks are a factor but makeup and a man's "bling-bling" comes off -- *everything that glitters isn't gold.* I treat the first initial date like test driving a car; I have rules that help me make my decision on whether or not that person should be entitled to a second date.

First Rule: Never let a salesman (suitor) push you into taking a test drive (date), only do it on your time. If you agree to a test drive make sure you're able to pick the place and control the duration and time of your date.

Second Rule: When taking the initial test drive, keep in mind that the opening conversation is usually a sales pitch. Just like you would stop a sales person to ask questions, rather than listening to his or her ramblings, stop and ask your date specific question(s). A person tends to only tell you the good about themselves if not prompted to do otherwise.

Third Rule: This is in correlation with the second rule -- Always check under the hood and check the mileage. In most cases, you're probably going to be test driving an old car, although it might run as good as new and it might be going for a bargain price, there's a big chance there are some hidden depreciations your seller may not point out. Do the proper inspections before attempting to drive it off the lot.

Fourth Rule: Let him/her know your desires if any; letting him/her know what you require and will or will not stand for eliminates the chances of a misunderstanding and either parties' time being wasted.

**Not everyone can handle bluntness, so express yourself in a firm but polite manner.*

Unlike real cars, there are no insurance coverage or factory warranties when seeking out a reliable make of men or women, so it's up to you to check the history. With that said I want you to write, tattoo if you have to, what I am about to state to you. **ALL APPLICANTS ARE NOT POTENTIAL HUSBANDS or WIVES!** The sooner you realize that all candidates are NOT potential husbands or wives, the easier it will be for you to just relax and *go with the flow*. Some people are just here as "fill-ins"-- practice for the real thing. Therefore, when dating, place no expectation on a person, this will allow room for growth and less disappointments in the long run. Just enjoy the ride for now…when it's time to reach your destination, your GPS will alert you.

First Date No No's

- First dates should never be at a home, not your house and especially not his.
- Do not excessively drink -- you do not want to make any decisions you wouldn't normally make sober.
- Avoid talk of past relationships -- this is a clear indication of baggage.
- Stay off the topic of sex -- I shouldn't have to tell you why you shouldn't talk about sex on a first date.
- If you're ready to cut the date short, voice that -- do yourself that favor.
- Do not add, follow, or send a social network friend request after the first date -- this comes off as too "thirsty" or needy.
- Don't get too touchy feely… brace yourself.
- Do not show up late. Be on time. Punctuality says a lot about your character.

- Do not complain - this only gives your date a preview of what's to come, nobody likes a complainer or nagger.
- Do not babble - tell him about yourself but not excessively. Let your date speak and just sit back and use your listening skills. Listen to what your date is telling you, not only to what he/she is saying but also to whatever they are trying to hide. Pay close attention to the body language; people unconsciously reveal a lot about themselves through body language alone.

"Expectation is resentment under construction" - Anne Lomatt

Now Accepting Applications

In my young adult years, I was always afraid to ask too many questions when on a date with a man because I was afraid he would think I'm prying too much and way too soon. In my later years, if I go on a date, and I don't ask questions, it's probably because I don't care to know the answers. To put it in layman's terms, I'm just not interested. In this day and age, it is safer to knock out the tough questions when in the early stages of dating -- think of it as a prescreening. Don't waste your time, ask questions before and during your initial first date. If all the baggage is laid out in the beginning, it gives you and that person an option to walk away free and clear, or stay and pursue even further. I've always viewed first dates like a job interview or a test drive; there has to be prescreening questions so that you can conclude whether or not that person is a good candidate for the position. I compiled a list below of obvious questions we commonly fail to ask for one reason or another.

1. ARE YOU SINGLE?
(You'd be surprised by the responses and how many people are dating while being involved with someone else.

2. What are you looking for? Serious relationship? Marriage? Just sex?

3. Do you have any kids? If so, how many?

4. Are you married? Have you ever been married? If so, how many times?

5. Have you ever been to jail or convicted of a crime?

6. Any medical conditions? (mental, sexually transmitted diseases, etc.) **This question may be more appropriate for the third or fourth date.*

7. What line of work are you in? (In this economy that's a nice

way of asking, Do you have a JOB?)

8. What are your short and long-term goals? Do you have a 5 and/or 10 year plan?

9. What's the craziest thing you've ever done?

10. What's the title of the last book you read, and how long ago did you read it?

11. What types of music do you listen to; what types of TV shows and movies do you watch? (This will give you a sense of what they're into.)

12. How is your relationship with your parents and siblings?

13. What are your religious beliefs?

14. What type of women/men do you usually go for?

15. Do you think that it's important for a man to take the lead in a relationship?

16. When was the last time you dated?

17. What is your first and last name? (Real name – a lot of people go by nicknames.)

18. What do you like to do for fun?

Yes, some of these questions are very bold, and I used to have a hard time asking them myself, until I realized I could have saved myself a lot of headaches if I asked the correct questions before my feelings started developing or before investing my time.

"Asking your date questions helps you determine what one's intentions and expectations are." – Seneca Ho Ken facebook

Caps Lock

The Right *One* vs. The Right one for Now

Every woman is looking for that perfect fit, and a lot of men are in search of the equivalent, which is why there are so many self-help books out there. Hundreds of dating sites promise to find you a mate based on personality analysis, but is there really a real secret to finding the right mate? Are you searching for love or are you waiting for the *right* person to fall in love with? Sometimes it's hard to differentiate between the two; too many people are in love with the *idea* of being in love -- they mistake anything that comes along for it. There's a huge difference between searching for love and waiting for the *right* person to fall in love *with*. When searching for love, you take whatever comes your way, when waiting for the *right* person to fall in love *with you*, the anticipation is still there, but there are other thought-out factors involved. When waiting, you don't settle for *right now's,* you wait for the *right one* because you know it's not just about falling for someone it's about falling together; it's knowing the other person wants a meaningful long-lasting relationship just as much as you do.

When you're dealing with someone, you can tell within the first few weeks whether or not this person is good for just *right now* or if this is someone you can see yourself with for the long run. People come in and out of our lives; some stay a while and others for just a brief moment. Some we become infatuated with while others we use just to kill time; everyone has their purpose. Sounds a bit harsh but hey, it is what it is. ***Don't try to turn the time killers into time keepers.***

The ones waiting for that right person sometimes have a mental checklist of what they want or desire in a life partner. I compiled a visual checklist below of some of the attributes and personality traits that I think are good characteristics to look for when considering a life partner. As the relationship gets deeper, you can check off each of the traits your partner possesses or add some traits of your own.

☑ THE CHECKLIST

- ☐ SENSITIVE
- ☐ CARING
- ☐ RELIABLE
- ☐ PROTECTIVE
- ☐ ATTENTIVE
- ☐ GENUINE
- ☐ AMBITIOUS
- ☐ HARD WORKER
- ☐ GOAL-ORIENTED
- ☐ CHALLENGES ME IN A GOOD WAY
- ☐ CAN BALANCE WORK, FAMILY & PERSONAL LIFE
- ☐ SELF CONTROL (NO SEX OUTSIDE OF THE RELATIONSHIP)
- ☐ LOVES WITH ***ACTION***
- ☐ INTELLIGENT
- ☐ EDUCATED
- ☐ CHARISMATIC

- ☐ SHARES THE SAME VALUES AND MORALS
- ☐ INTEGRITY
- ☐ HUMBLE
- ☐ GOD-FEARING
- ☐ COMMITTED
- ☐ GOOD COMMUNICATOR
- ☐ HONEST
- ☐ TRUSTWORTHY
- ☐ APPRECIATIVE
- ☐ SUPPORTIVE
- ☐ HUMOROUS
- ☐ FLEXIBLE
- ☐ ADAPTABLE
- ☐ SPONTANEOUS
- ☐ GOOD FAMILY VALUES
- ☐ OUTGOING
- ☐ SKILLED AROUND THE HOUSE/HANDY

- ☐ LOVES CHILDREN
- ☐ PASSIONATE
- ☐ COMPASSIONATE
- ☐ UNDERSTANDING
- ☐ GREAT LISTENER
- ☐ A GENTLEMEN / A LADY
- ☐ CHIVALROUS
- ☐ SINCERE
- ☐ LOYAL
- ☐ UNSELFISH
- ☐ STABLE
- ☐ GREAT SEX (Just Keeping It Real)
- ☐ GENEROUS

*When it's real it's **real**, you won't have to look for love; love will find you.*

Mr. and Mrs. "Fake" Believe

Finding real love in a world of "fake believe" seems like an almost impossible task. If only dating was as easy as pressing a "Like" or Dislike button on facebook or as easy as asking your followers for a background check on your dating prospects. Unfortunately, finding Mr. or Mrs. Right is not that easy, but everything good is worth working for. From a realistic standpoint…no one is unflawed, and there is no such thing as a fairytale ending. Fairytales are shit made stories that fool you into having and focusing on unrealistic expectations instead of the actual fact that nothing is perfect. People run from a relationship at the slightest indication of inconsistency or inconvenience. You have to be willing to fight for it -- or create something original. Here are a few relationship faux pas:

Entitlements

One of the most common mistakes we make when choosing a mate is bestowing him/her with a higher title. People do the craziest things when they believe they're entitled to something. Crowning someone before their time only stunts their growth. Some women tend to treat their man like a king by giving him wife privileges right from the very beginning of the relationship. Yes, he was charming enough to win you over, but that only classifies him as a prince for now. Let him work his way up to earning the title of your king rather than prematurely crowning him. The same goes for men, putting a women on a pedestal doesn't qualify her as a queen, she has to earn her title as well.

When people earn a title, they feel they deserve the praise and admiration that comes along with that entitlement. They also recognize the responsibilities and obligations that come with it. Having ***justification gives a certain gratification*** -- it gives a person reason to go over and beyond what is expected of them.

"A man calling me Baby right off the bat is a turn off to me... I like to earn my title. This way I'll know for sure I am your only Baby." - @KillHershey twitter

"I don't want it right now, let me earn it... That way I'll forever understand its value." - @IamBranding twitter

Sex-suscitation

Your relationship has bitten the poisonous apple and just like that, the romance is dead. Every time you and your significant other have a fight, your solution is to just have make-up sex -- excluding the making up part. The problems start to build and build, and as a result, people seek out sex/relationship therapists, books and advice from friends to figure out how to mend the connection. Here's a tip...You cannot fuck the life back into a relationship; a failing relationship needs more than sex to revive it. You need a resurrection serum, and the ingredients to this serum are communication, communication and more communication. Not being able to fully convey what you dislike or disapprove of, for fear of it hurting your partner's feelings or starting an argument is the basis of a lot of relationship problems, whether it's in the bedroom or not. Unsettled arguments trickle down to the bedroom, so clear the air. Keeping an open floor for discussions and criticism is one way to sort out those bedroom issues. Communication is a part of romance -- therefore romance is more than sex, romance is the prerequisite to *good* sex -- not just sexual positions and climaxes, it is everything you do prior to making love.

Dreaming

Remember when you were a child and your parents would send you to bed and instead of following orders you would just go into your room and play around until you heard footsteps heading towards your door? When they would open the door, you would squeeze your eyes shut and pretend you were sleeping and sometimes if they stood by the door long enough, you would unconsciously fall asleep? Well, a lot of people are in that type of relationship, fighting to stay awake but failing miserably. When it comes to relationships, you cannot "fake it till you make it;" it takes ***"doing it and pursuing it"*** to succeed -- but not many people can achieve relationship success. Too many people get caught up in just the dream of a perfect relationship that we forget to wake up and work on the reality -- thus turning it into a nightmare. We work at everything else so why not work at creating our own reality of a beautiful daydream?

"Never take for granted the power that exists in listening." - Darius Jefferson facebook

"Intimacy without communication is like icing without the cake. First it feels good, but then it ends up making us sick." - David Manuel facebook

"Love is another 9-5 with unpaid overtime and great benefits but, you have to read the application before you sign up. You can still get fired on your day off." - Xavier Warner facebook

"Too many people are in relationships just to say they're in a relationship. When did a relationship become the new must-have fashion accessory?" - Claudia Versailles facebook

Dating Mr. *Potential*

What some of us fail to realize is that when we hold on to unhealthy situations, not only are we hurting the other person for selfish reasons, we hurt ourselves in the process. For every action there's a reaction and whatever we project, the universe will find a way to set it in motion. Towards the end of my last relationship, a mutual friend of both Mr. Black and I asked, "What exactly did you see in Mr. Black that made you think that he was such a good guy? Why did you go so hard for him, was it potential you saw or something else? Why did you hold on for so long?"

Those had to be some of the realest questions I've been asked. Was it potential? Why did I go so hard for him? What exactly did I see in him? And why did I stick around for as long as I did? While I couldn't figure out how to answer him, I replied vaguely, "I think he blinded me with his dick game," -- but that was only part of the truth. I officially met "Mr. Black" back in 2007, and what most attracted me to him was his ambition and drive. He told me his dreams of starting his own athletic training business, and I did whatever I could to support those dreams, even if it meant that I wouldn't be included in the reality. I understood our mutual friend's question quite clearly, but I didn't want to fall into the category of women that turn men into pet projects. The women that say "I can work with this" or "I can change him." At the end of the day, you cannot change a man unless he is willing and ready to be changed— or he changes on his own. Change starts from within, so yes, potential was why I stuck around. I saw the big picture…but later on realized what I was doing was making him a better man for whomever comes after me. Toward the end, the only thing that seemed to bond us was his startup business. We had a common goal -- making him successful.

Even though I had a startup business of my own, I took a lot of time out to focus on his goals. But I came to recognize that I didn't only fall into the "I can work with this" statistic, it seemed as though I was the leader of the whole movement. Putting my goals and dreams aside, so I could help him achieve his -- and he allowed me to do so without the intentions of helping me with my own.

Some of us get caught up in an idealized image of someone rather than taking the time out to learn the actual person. We get caught up in *what* that person is instead of *who* they are -- I know I've been a victim of my expectations. I meet a man that looks great on paper but is worth less than a paper plane. People only *tell* you what they want you to see, but *if they show you early on who they really are…believe them.* I have learned to be a watcher of actions rather than drawing and painting conclusions from what I hear. Sometimes even your eyes can deceive you, so you have to tap into your super powers and use x-ray vision (gut and intuition) to see past the bullshit. Looking back on the whole thing I know now that not every support system can work as well as Obama and Michelle's, and I've come to terms with that. You cannot give away too much of "you" –leave some of "you" for yourself. In the end although my heart wanted to fight to make things work, I had to release myself from that situation.

"A lot of women lack discernment. A lot of women see suit, car, his age, occupation, or position...and assume that equates to his character and/or the way he will treat her. I know many fantastic women…that choose dumb-ass guys. Being a good man/woman doesn't counter a bad choice." - Jullian Goodin facebook

Unhappily Married

Mark has been married for five years and has two beautiful daughters and a beautiful home as a result. Every time he and his lovely family would come to town to visit, I would insist that they stay with me so that I could spend some time with the girls. I've never seen a happier young married couple; it seemed they had it all figured out. Now here's where I start spilling all of this man's business…one day I received a phone call from Mark's wife -- which was very out of the ordinary because I am so accustomed to hearing from Mark and rarely from his wife, Jane. I was so wrapped up in a meeting that I let the call go to voicemail. Now, I am not big on checking voice messages -- although I was very curious to know the nature of her call, the message went unheard because of other distractions.

Weeks later while scrolling down my facebook timeline, I noticed some subliminal back and forth going on between Mark and his wife, and photos of him and a new woman popped up in his timeline. Concerned and a bit nosey, I decided to call him and asked, "What's going on? Why are you venting on Facebook?" "I left Jane," he flagrantly said, "Um what do you mean you left Jane? You mean you guys separated?," I asked, "… no, just what I said -- I left her…I met a woman at a friend's BBQ, we slept together that very night and the next week I left and moved in with Molly," he said shamelessly. I was dumbstruck. I tried to convince him that he was making a terrible mistake, tried to get him to see that temporary pleasure sometimes leads to permanent consequences -- I'm paraphrasing here of course -- but no matter how much I pleaded, I just couldn't get through to him. Months later while browsing through Instagram photos, I noticed his photo captions where noticeably depressing, so once again I picked up the phone to check up on him. "Hey, what's going on? … you do realize photo captions speak volumes right…What's got you so depressed?" I asked. "Well Molly and I broke up…I asked her to move out, but before you judge me let me explain." "Okay, I'm listening," I replied -- he goes on to tell me that what I and other people don't realize is that him and his wife were having marital problems long before Molly came into the picture. That he was unhappy for a very long time, and Molly made him realize that. The first few months of their relationship were perfect but things got rough when his wife (separated) put him on child support and attempted to start a custody battle. He lost his car, job and couldn't stay afloat and that's when he started to see Molly's true colors. His financial situation was putting a strain on his new relationship, so although he truly loves Molly, he knew things wouldn't work out -- he eventually had to vacate his new apartment and move back in with his wife. I told him, "Well that's very big of Jane because I would have never taken you back!" "Well to be honest with you, if it wasn't for my financial problems I wouldn't be here…I would still be with Molly. I plan on staying here until I get back on my feet and then I'm leaving again…I am not happy here, I don't know why Jane keeps trying to make this work. For the life of me, I can't get her to understand the simple fact that I don't want to be with her!" he said bitterly. Taken back, I replied, "Well she wants things to work out because she loves you, Mark." "She loves me? Why love me if I don't love her? I don't understand her logic, and I can't get her to understand mine…how do I get her to understand? I've tried to tell her how I feel and for some reason she won't get it!" Mark replied.

So here's what I suggested –

Release her…A person can't help who they love and in this case, Jane is not going to believe she can't rekindle or fix the marriage when you guys are living under the same roof. If conversations are not helping you get your point across or you can't get through to her, write a letter. No not an email -- or text; text messages leave too much room for interpretation. Do it the old-fashioned way, with a handwritten letter -- this makes it more personal and will help emphasize how serious you are about the matter. Chances are, she will read and re-read this letter, and the words will imprint and sink in. This is also a better method than you getting up and leaving without warning… a considerate release.

Dear J, *Letter*

Allow me to elaborate on the effectiveness of writing a letter. Notice how people take things to heart when they accidentally overhear someone talking about them, whether it's the truth or not -- that person will sit down and dissect every single word, even down to the tone you used when you stated your distaste. Use this effect to your advantage; sometimes it doesn't matter how many times you tell a person what s/he's doing wrong…they'll just see it as nagging. As long as you haven't fully walked away from a relationship s/he'll assume they're doing something right -- since you're still around. If you just can't seem to get through to your significant other about a subject you find very important or difficult to explain verbally -- write him/her a ***Dear J** letter*. The point is to write a letter as though you are writing to a friend or confidante; this letter should be written as though you are just venting to a friend and as if this was never intended to be seen by your significant other. When writing this letter, make sure you are not nagging and pointing fingers, remember for every action there is a reaction…do more stating then blaming, but be sure to state your faults as well. People are more accepting and receptive when they think they're not the only person at fault. Be sure to indicate your emotional standpoint on the subject, the more emotions you reveal the deeper it will sink in.

SIDENOTE: Do this as tastefully as possible, take great consideration for your partner's feelings -- Remember some words can't be taken back.

Safety Net

A lot of you are afraid to let someone out of your life, because of the fear that you'll miss out on another human being's destiny. Let's explore this concept: Brian, a successful businessman is friends with an aspiring singer named Amy; Amy has a crush on Brian. Now, Brian knows this, but continues to let Amy's feelings get stronger. Amy wants more than a friendship, and Brian knows this because Amy is voicing her frustration to Brian. She now wants to spend time and be more involved in Brian's life. Brian is just not interested in Amy romantically, and wants to pull away from the friendship -- but what's holding Brian back? Not the fear that he would lose out on a good friendship, because at this point, Amy's antics are becoming an annoyance and adding stress in Brian's life. What's really holding Brian back is the fear of losing out on Amy's future, that "what if" factor. A lot of us suffer from the "what if" factor, what if Amy actually does live out her dreams and break into the recording industry? Yes, Brian wants a little taste of the limelight or maybe a ride on Amy's coattails.

We see this same scenario not only in friendships but also in relationships: Tanya has been dating Travis, her high school sweetheart, for four years. Throughout these four years, both Tanya and Travis have had sexual relations outside of the relationship. The trust was gone which in turn caused numerous arguments and fights, but rather then break it off and start fresh with someone totally new, Tanya keeps on holding on to Travis – **Pause --** Did I mention Travis was a star college football player?...You see where I'm going with this? Here's where Tanya and Travis almost have a fairytale ending, even though they had a lot of stress weighing down the relationship. Travis actually makes it into the NFL. All that holding on actually did pay off for Tanya. She now has a full meal ticket! Unfortunately for her though, she ended up with just a happy meal because Travis got injured in the start of the season and you can guess what happened next— DING DING DING! <The Breakup for 200 please> that's correct! Tanya dropped the safety net (Travis) and went back to doing what she does best.

One-lationship

Meagan was in what I call a *One-lationship*. Before I go into this scenario, allow me to elaborate -- a *One-lationship* is being in a relationship where only one partner acknowledges the fact that they are in a relationship; the other partner is only there for the physical aspect (the sex) but is lacking in all other areas; a "One Way Street" type of relationship. Continuing from where I left off, Meagan gave and gave and gave, and her boyfriend Adam took and took and took. She didn't only give herself up emotionally and physically, she gave materially and financially also. At first, Meagan couldn't quite figure out where she was going wrong in the relationship because Adam found cunning ways to manipulate her. Meagan is selfless and finds more joy in giving then receiving, and Adam took full advantage of these weaknesses. *I refer to these attributes as weaknesses because I believe that any and everything that can be used against you is a disadvantage; whether it's love, selflessness, religion or any other seemingly harmless dynamic.*

It started off with Meagan purchasing one or two decorative pieces for his place. When purchasing, Adam would recite one of the many lines *users* like to recite "I'll pay you back." Next, he advanced to giving her clues on what he wanted or supposedly was going to purchase, but just couldn't find time to do— because work wouldn't permit it. So before the purchases, he would help pick out the items, and when it came time for him to give his final approval and the funds to make the purchase, he would disappear and later claim something came up. Decorative furnishing, clothing, electronics -- Meagan even helped him pay off some of his school loans and a security deposit for a rental condo. Things were getting too expensive, and Meagan felt more like a sugar momma then a girlfriend. When Meagan finally got hip to Adam's game plan she addressed the issue, and he fed her another one of those *user* lines in defense, "I never asked you to do any of those things, you took it upon yourself to do it."

In life there are givers and there are takers; it's rare that you find someone that is balanced. We all play a different role in each relationship we enter. In one relationship you might be submissive, but after being unappreciated you may leave that relationship and when entering the next situation, you may switch up your role and decide to get rid of that apron and broom until a more deserving man earns those husband privileges.

Accept the fact that not everyone means well -- users, abusers, takers, etc. Everyone doesn't deserve a ride or die woman/man; be very selective when choosing who's riding with you. In Meagan's case, she played the woman that helped Adam refine himself; yes in the end she was disappointed things didn't work out but she's not alone -- a lot of other women have been the woman that helped refine a man for that next woman that comes into his life. That may be the role you have to play, learn from it and move on. You gain knowledge from every experience. Now that you know better, you should seek better -- your next should always be better than your last.

Friend Box

One of the most common questions single women ask is → Where are all the good men? -- Well, I have a simple answer—most of the good men are in the friend box (or zone) that we intentionally put them in. When meeting available men, I have a habit of doing one of these two things: 1) put them in a friend box or 2) try to fix them up with other single women I know. It's not until it's too late that I realize how much of a good guy that person is. I had one guy tell me, "I'm a great guy, and I'm confident that this is fact not fiction, you're trying to pass me off to another woman…If you do this to every good guy you meet what are you left with?" That was some food for thought for me, and it caused me to start re-evaluating the men I put in the friend zone.

You heard the quote by George Moore that reads, "A man travels the world in search of what he needs and returns home to find it." What do you think he meant by that? A relationship built on friendship makes for a better foundation. Sometimes you have to stop searching, so you can find what's right under your nose.

Some of us are so clever that we put a man in the friend box without him noticing it; we allow him to do all the things a boyfriend is supposed to do like take us to the movies, dinner… pay for gifts etc. Sometimes he even does more than that man you've "been running after" does. In his mind, each grand gesture he makes gets him one step closer to making you his woman and to you, he is *just a friend.* You're selfishly allowing his feelings to build for you without any intentions of reciprocating any feelings. Leading someone on without any intentions of reciprocating their feelings or emotions is equivalent to ordering off of the *"Fuck Me Side of the Menu"* and being surprised when he actually tries to sleep with you… just upsetting. Nobody likes to be led on; if he is just a friend, let him know that sooner than later.

SIDENOTE: The *"Fuck Me Side of the Menu"* is the most expensive side of a dinner menu.

***DOUBLE SIDENOTE:** If your male friend is doing more for you than your significant other is doing… It's time to trade your significant other in or replace him with an upgrade.

You Say He's Just A Friend *... (with Benefits)*

No such thing as friends with benefits…casual or meaningless sex with a friend is anything but casual; one of the parties involved is bound to grow some kind of an emotional attachment. Having all the benefits of having a boy/girlfriend without the title can be lethal for a friendship. For men, it's easier because it can be purely physical, for women it is barely beneficial because the "majority" of women's hearts are attached to their vaginas. Having sex with a male friend is like being a sexual cannibal, a black widow spider; the only difference is instead of you eating and killing your male sex partner you'll be killing a friendship. You can be just sex buddies or just friends, but mixing the two never ends well. Keep in mind that sex buddy is still another form of commitment because you are giving your body to someone on a regular. Mixing sex with friendship can be very toxic and poisonous without the right antidote or treatment.

Antidote: *The only way you can suppress feelings or emotions is by constantly having conversations about other people either of you are seeing and setting boundaries. Never let the other participant think or believe they are the only person in the picture; this will only throw off the balance -- constantly talk about the other people you are dating and the status of your arrangement. This is not a foolproof solution, so if you truly value your friendship, don't add any confusion. Keep it strictly platonic.*

The Absence of Nothing is... NOTHING

Donna has been seeing Marvin on and off for a little over three years…from day one to now, nothing has changed except the dates on the calendar. Her previous relationship before this one was almost close to perfect, but due to a series of events, they had to part ways. Donna went into her current situation expecting more than the last because she got to experience firsthand what it felt like to be in a healthy relationship prior to the one she's in now. When you're accustomed to the best, you expect better than the rest…but in this case Donna decided to settle for the lesser. While speaking to Donna about the situation, she said something particularly alarming to me. She said, "I don't even know what we are?" I asked her, "What do you mean? You guys have been together for 3 years?" She then went on to say "He has never asked me to be his girlfriend, and every time I bring it up, he claims I'm nagging. We break up over the same things over and over again, well…I don't even know if I should call it a break up since he refuses to make things official. He says, 'I promise I'll change… make a list of demands, and I'll try my best to work on them' But all he gives me is empty words, he just doesn't follow through with action -- things will be good for about a week, but then it goes back to the same old routine. He gives me nothing…no dates or outings, no compliments or a gesture of appreciation, no real 1-on-1 time…even the sex is not what it used to be. I'm giving him so much of myself and receiving very little in return but still -- my heart keeps me here, in hopes things will change…My confidence is shot, and this man keeps draining my energy! It's to the point where if he asks me to go to a fast food restaurant, I'll get excited because it's so out of the ordinary."

What Marvin is doing here is conditioning Donna to accept less than she requires; a person will test the waters just to see how much you'll let them get away with. You instill certain treatment by what you gradually permit. In other words, if you allow the minimal performance or lack of follow-through, then that's just what you'll receive. Men don't love the way women do. Men fall in love/like through happiness they feel while most women fall in love/like through happiness they give.

Recondition yourself— strip down all your insecurities. Insecurities build the need to prove yourself to others all the time. Staying with a man that is not doing his part to make you feel secure is not loyalty or love; it's insecurity. You should not desire to be in a relationship more than the other person does, there has to be a balance. Have you ever heard the phrase *"He who loves less, wins?"* -- as selfish and juvenile as that sounds, this statement is observably true. It's usually the one that is willing to go the extra mile and eager to do whatever it takes for the other person that ends up being the injured party.

Think about what you require, not what you want. Stop auditioning. You're made to play the leading woman just not in his movie -- ***wait for the man, that instead of casting you for a role, he builds the script around your character.*** No need to fight to be in someone's life; a man has to want to deserve you, want to earn your approval. Simply put, if he doesn't fully love you enough to commit by now, then chances are he will never make that commitment…cut and dry -- there is no such thing as half-assed love, he has to be willing to go all the way with you. If a man is not afraid of losing you…Run the other way…don't chase him down.

You're not going to miss out on anything when you leave -- The absence of nothing is…NOTHING! He didn't do shit for you when he was there, so what is there to miss? The answer is… Nothing! So release nothing and embrace everything -- if the wrong man/men made you feel right, imagine the capabilities the right man has. So abandon that one-lationship and prepare yourself for a REALationship -- a relationship between "two equally committed individuals.

The only people you need in your life are the ones that prove they need you in theirs." – Unknown facebook

"Give the best to the one that brings out the best in you." - @KillHershey twitter

"Stop Settling! Not only do you devalue yourself, you give the person you're settling for a false sense of accomplishment!" - @BaisdenLive twitter

"Recognize your worth and you never have to beg anyone for their attention. You will never have to belittle yourself to get people to notice you. The problem nowadays is that so many people fail to understand their worth. They allow these TV shows and ignorant celebrity icons to define their existence. You have to know your worth to get your worth. I myself have also been a victim of following the path of someone else's definition of what I should be. But in order to teach a nation you must build the nation within, and that's the first test in understanding how to love others, and capture the essence of others worth. You must know yours first, I hope you know you're beautiful☺"- Vincent Moore facebook

Catch and Release

Sometimes we allow someone to stay in our lives a lot longer than they should be because of one selfish reason or another. Some women are afraid to leave a relationship because they are waiting for the other person to leave first, no matter how unhealthy the relationship is. They stick around because they are just too scared to make the first move. It may be loyalty, but I doubt it; it's a mixture of spinelessness and the fear of being alone and starting over. You need that attachment no matter how unhealthy it is…it defines you. Maybe you're afraid of another woman cashing out on your investment; or it's the sex that's keeping you from letting him go. Relationships, friendships, situations all have expiration dates. Sometimes holding onto that person prevents you from giving anyone else an actual chance. You must learn how to let go of those that are already gone.

I had a situation where I was caught in limbo. I wanted to date other people because my prior relationship had reached its expiration date, but I always found myself running back to him. I would agree to go on a date with a new suitor, and on my way to meet up with my date, the guy I was stuck in the state of indeterminateness with would send me a simple "How are you doing?" text, and I would immediately park the car and respond with, "Missing you, what are you doing now?" One text would lead to another, and I would end up at his place instead of going on my initial date.

It wasn't that I couldn't just get up and leave at any time; it was because a particular part of the sex was too damned good to give up. I was too afraid to throw that fish back in the pond because I was too selfish to "willingly" let any other woman experience, feel or enjoy what I had experienced. What I eventually found out was other women were in fact sampling my catch whether I liked it or not. Good sex will do that to you, but I eventually threw that fish back into the pond and to my surprise found that there where bigger, better fish to catch… and fry.

Ending a relationship entirely is an essential step to starting something fresh, release the clutter and open up to being caught by someone new.

Social Network Release Tip: Delete your ex from all of your social network accounts. It may come across as petty, but while a lot of us like to stay connected and know what the ex is up to, you don't need a constant reminder of what went wrong. Deleting your ex from your social accounts will allow you to heal at a much faster rate. Later when you feel you are over the situation, you can add him/her again; if he or she isn't petty, they will understand and accept your request. Think about your emotions and how things are affecting you before thinking about how it'll make you look.

STOP dating continuations of your last mate

Right now I'm sitting here and I promise you, I can hear Jamie Foxx's voice in my head singing, "I swear I always fall for your type." I've fallen for that type a time or two, but there comes a time in your life when you realize that -- *just good enough* isn't at all good for you -- this isn't the right fit. Stop trying him on and wait for the one that's tailor made for you.

Joyce complained about always being used and not being able to find a man that would take her seriously for more than a few weeks. Joyce felt she needed to feel loved and was ready for a real relationship. One evening while getting dressed at my house for a girl's club night out Joyce says, "As good as I look in this dress... I better find a man tonight!" I turned and looked at her with a straight face and said, "See that's your problem there, you're always prowling for men on the wrong hunting ground."

What a lot of women fail to realize is while we do the choosing, the men do the closing. By closing I mean we leave it up to the man to finalize the deal. Where you choose to do the choosing, reflect on the quality of the catch. If you're continually looking for men in the clubs, you will continually find the continuation of the last man you met in a club. Let me point out one well-known fact, MEN DO NOT GO TO THE CLUB IN SEARCH OF A WIFE, they go to the club to find a woman, maybe even two women to fornicate with. Don't take this personally, it is what it is. If you continue to fish in the same pond, you are almost always guaranteed the same catch, remember the bait always dies, so be mindful of what you use to capture a man's attention. Change your scenery, and you'll change the type of men you encounter. Simple. ***Relationships are not trilogies; you've read that book before put it down and move on to a different genre.***

"The fishermen can't be upset about the type of fish they catch. Check your bait; certain fish are attracted to specific bait." - Craig Paul Moore, Jr. facebook

CONFESS to PROGRESS

Most of us have been hurt in one way or another and we carry that baggage into new relationships. So you tell yourself

"I've been hurt before so I have to keep my walls up now."

"I've been cheated on so I don't think I can trust another man."

"I've been abused mentally and physically and I don't think I can take anymore."

"I invested way too much in my last relationship and saw no return."

Erykah Badu said it best in her lyrics for "Bag Lady" when she said:

Bag lady you gon hurt your back
Draggin all them bags like that.
I guess nobody ever told you how
You must hold on to issue, issue issue

One day all them bags gon get in your way
One day all them bags gon get in your way
I said one day all them bags gon get in your way

So pack light, hooo hooo

Bag lady you gon miss your bus
You can't hurry up cause you got too much stuff
When they see you comin they just take off runnin
From you, it's true, oh yes they dooo

One day he gon say you crowdin my space
One day he gon say you crowdin my space
I said one day he gon say you crowdin my space

So pack light yeah yea yea yea yea yeah

Girl I know
Sometimes it's hard and we can't let go

Ooh if someone hurts you o so bad inside
And you can't deny it you can't slip by it
Sooooooo if you still breathin
Oooo oooo ooooooo
Ooooo ooooo oooooooooo

So where my garbage bag lady
Let it go let it go let it go let it go
And what about the grocery bag lady
I bet ya love could make it better
Im talkin to my Gucci bag ladies
Let it go let it go let it go let it go
And what about my paper sack ladies
I bet ya love could make it better
What about my nickel bag ladies
Let it go let it go let it go let it go
Light pack when ya pack ya bags ladies
Bet ya love could make it better

Bad relationships only help you refine yourself. I took the time out to thank one of my ex's for the lessons I learned and assured him that "when the next deserving man enters my life, wherever I went wrong with you -- I will make it my purpose to do right by him -- you have not ruined me…just know that." I learn to reprogram myself and walk away from each situation with a system upgrade. Stop carrying around unneeded data and Re-boot, Re-program and Upgrade your software.

Speak or Write Down Your Regrets…Get Over It and **LET IT GO!**

"Stop letting people ride on your emotional train of thought, without paying the proper fare" - @KillHershey

"I am reminded daily….To let go isn't to forget, not think about, or ignore. It doesn't leave feelings of anger, jealousy, or regret. Letting go isn't winning, and it isn't losing. It's not about pride, it's

not about how you appear, and it's not obsessing or dwelling on the past. Letting go isn't blocking memories or thinking sad thoughts, it doesn't leave emptiness, hurt or sadness. It's not giving in or giving up. Letting go isn't about loss, and it's not defeat. To let go is to cherish memories, but to overcome and to move on. It is having an open mind and confidence in the future. Letting go is accepting. It is learning and experiencing and growing. To let go is to be thankful for the experiences that made you laugh, made you cry and made you grow. It's about all that you have, all that you had and all that you will soon gain. Letting go is having the courage to accept change, and the strength to keep moving. Letting go is growing up. It is realizing that the heart can sometimes be the most potent remedy. To let go is to open a door, to clear a path and to set yourself free." – Nathan Fragelus

facebook

LET IT GO!

The relationship is over -- whether it was his fault or yours, don't overanalyze it. The important thing to do right now is get over it as soon as possible, no need to torture yourself with the "what ifs", the whys and why nots. The reality of the matter is things didn't work out...now "Let It Go." Yeah I know...That's easier said than done, but the more you tell yourself to let it go the easier it will be to start the reconditioning process.

RECONDITIONING AFTER A BREAKUP

Recognize your fears, insecurities and anxieties -- you always hear "the first step to fixing a problem is recognizing or admitting you have one." This is also true with relationships. Accept the inevitable -- you can't control everything; some circumstances are beyond your control. Say to yourself, "It is what it is, and so be it...I'm letting it go." You are only responsible for your actions, well being and your happiness; everything else is out of your hands. Forgive yourself and re-focus your energy and attention—remind yourself of the priorities in your life. Rewire your thoughts and frame of mind. After a breakup, we sometimes feel hurt, broken, and for some of us; even lost. We often think that we will never love or give ourselves fully to another and some start to think that they are damaged goods or maybe too far gone. We search externally for someone or something to make us happy instead of looking for the happiness within. Don't let anyone steal your joy; you have to stop and acknowledge your inner power, strength, and love. Failing to do so is a form of self- sabotage, stop compromising yourself...if you are lost, find yourself. Forget about your past relationship(s) and try to move on with the new.

"Let the past bury its dead" - Henry Wadsworth Longfellow

BONUS TIP: Reprogram his number in your phone to "LET IT GO." These are three little words, but a big step in the right direction. If you won't need his number in the future (for business, kids, etc.), delete his contacts all together; if you know you might need it, write it down somewhere and then delete it from your phone, so you won't be tempted to call, text, or email him in desperation. Don't reprogram his name to anything negative -- that will only build more resentment and keep you in the negative. "Let It Go" is an appropriate title because it will serve as a reminder to Let It Go. Let what go? "It"... Not "him" or the breakup. Let everything go; the pain, hurt, anger, resentment, the whole ordeal... LET IT GO!

Last and most important: Repetition— just as repetition is true with propaganda, it is also true with breaking a habit or emotional tie. If you continuously tell yourself; let it go, let it go, let it go, your mind and inner self will allow you to do just that...LET IT GO!

"Don't let the past steal your present" Cherrie L. Moraga

"Every time you break up with someone, you get one step closer to the right one. You should look at moving on as getting closer to meeting the one." – Unknown

Alt

Principle of Replacement

After a bad break-up we've all gone through a point in our lives where we were at a standstill or at our breaking point. It is important to remember -- though you might not feel it at the moment…It is always darkest before the dawn. I always tell myself a breakthrough is right around the corner. Inspiration comes in many forms; if you're going through hurt or pain, turn those emotions into inspiration. Turn that energy into something creative. When dating, there are no relationship insurance plans or policies that can protect you from getting your heart broken, and you can't get paid time-and-half for pulling a double shift. If you have pre-existing conditions, most insurance companies wouldn't cover you anyway. So you just have to take a loss when you've been demoted from a position.

Bouncing Back Tips:

- Write or develop something that you can share with others.
- Do not romanticize the bad -- if the bad outweighs the good, a breakup was inevitable.
- Make a list of friendly or motivational reminders of why the relationship was hazardous.
- Get rid of any emotional triggers, anything that reminds you of that person.
- We all make mistakes; the trick is to make better mistakes.
- Do not focus on the coulda, shoulda— clear your mind and start with the GONNA. The where do I go from here?
- Make happy changes— Happy choices equals happy changes -- Do better. Get better. Move on to BETTER.
- Use the principle of replacement -- remove one thought by replacing it with another. It's hard to remove something completely, so the trick is not to concentrate on removing but replacing or substituting those unwanted thoughts with completely new ones and following those thoughts up with positive actions—we are our thoughts.
- Prioritize your goals -- set your goals in order of importance.

Let your aspirations keep you busy.

Deliberately Single

One of the common misconceptions people have is when a person is single, they're miserable or thirsty for love or maybe even crazy. Sometimes single is another term for "just doing me." Not everyone needs a partner or relationship to justify or define them. Nowhere in the dictionary's definition of the word *single* do you find the words miserable or unhappy. Being single is not a plague or a death sentence, and no it doesn't mean you have a defect. Sometimes it's a choice; there are people out there that are *deliberately single*.

Being deliberately single means you consciously made the decision to be or stay single for one reason or another. To some, being single means less distractions and being able to get up and go, whenever. Being single means being independent and liberated, it means not having to check in with anyone or having to be asked, "Where are you?" "Who are you with?" "What are you doing?" Being single means no one is slowing or holding you down and you are free to see who you want, when you want. Being single means you are just feeling things out, weighing your options -- and most importantly, being single means you're getting to know yourself, you're taking the time out to love YOU better—finding, exploring and deciding what you want in a partner. When you take time out to focus on "self" and/or your highest purpose, everything else will follow.

"Single only means unhappy to the person who is already unhappy with themselves. My thinking is that being single should come naturally. To be in a relationship, on the other hand, is a choice. I am single because no one has come along that inspires me to want to choose otherwise." - Jacqueline Diamond facebook

"I'm single because I was born that way." - Mae West

"When a man finds a woman, he finds a good thing, but a lot of these women out here are not worth the headaches...Get money

and get married at 40 is my motto" - Tarique Sb facebook

"Welcome loneliness if it gives you peace of mind. If any kind of relationship does not make you want to be a better person, then you simply do not need it" - David Manuel facebook

"When I see people who have just gotten out of a relationship go right back into another relationship, it tells me one of two things about them. Either they were already seeing the other person they got right into a relationship with while they were with the previous person, or they really didn't care for the previous person as much as they made that person think they did. It takes time to get over the shock of being separated from someone you say you really care about and love. The easier it is to go to the next person, the less you cared." - David E. Goodin facebook

"You got to first learn to stand on your own before you can be a contributing partner." - @MsCarolModa twitter

"The worst loneliness -- the kind you can't escape from -- is when you are uncomfortable with yourself." - @MsSoncerae twitter

IMPROVE SELF←→IMPROVE CIRCUMSTANCES

Everyone is searching for that better half, but it is important that you're a better whole before you can share a slice of that whole with a significant other. In other words, you have to be a better "you" before you can better someone else. This he/she completes me bullshit is getting redundant, fuck what Jerry Maguire says, NOBODY COMPLETES YOU! A person can only inspire you, he or she can never complete you; you alone can do that. Knowing what you are good at or what you possess -- and accepting yourself completely will aid you in putting things into perspective.

I hear from a lot of people that it's difficult for them to find a good mate; if you improve yourself, you will improve your circumstances and the chances of finding that person that's right for you increases. Investing in yourself is the best investment you can ever make. You have to be willing to invest in *YOU* -- by doing so you will be adding value to yourself -- thus allowing your stock to go up. If you want the best, you have to be the best before seeking out the best.

"You can't sweep other people off their feet, if you can't be swept off your own." - Clarence Day

Take a moment to write down a list of areas you have to work on. Writing down your problem areas shows your willingness to improve and will also serve as a form of affirmation. Write exactly what you would like to improve and the steps it will take to make those improvements. The universe has a way of giving you exactly what you put out there; think of this as a letter you are writing to the universe.

Once you start working on these specific areas in your life and manage to improve some, go back to your list and revise it. You may choose to just cross out every area you conquered; this way you can see your progress over time.

Commit to your goals before committing to a mate.

When entering a relationship, your goals and dreams should never be compromised. Put yourself at the top of your very own list. When setting goals, prioritizing is very important. Make a list of goals you would like to accomplish starting with what's most important or what's the hardest to achieve. I say the hardest to reach because when you conquer your hardest goal or start with the end in mind, everything else seems to fall into place more easily.

- **Go After it!** Writing down these goals is only the first step; you cannot sit around and just wait for someone to knock on your door with what you requested. In other words, your goals can not be placed for delivery…you have to visualize it then go after it.
- **Completion Date:** Set a finish date for each goal; this doesn't mean you'll have to abandon a goal if you don't meet the deadline. Scheduling a completion date only helps to motivate you; there is no expiration date for goals and dreams.
- **Keep Tabs of Your Surroundings:** You may also want to write down the people and things in your life that can help you accomplish these goals.

SIDENOTE: Always, I mean ALWAYS take time out to celebrate your small victories. This will serve as motivation for your future goals, whether it is a movie, a cupcake or a spa date with yourself, make sure you take time out to enjoy your accomplishment and congratulate yourself.

One of the positive things about social networks is the motivational and positive comments you can get when you set out to meet a goal and you post it on your timeline. Starting a video blog on YouTube and sharing it on your social network feeds is a great way to find motivation and inspiration from others also. Not only are you sharing your journey, you'll also get to hear people's stories and maybe even inspire others to join you on your exploration.

Examples: *My 60 Day Challenge to Get A Revenge Body*; *My 60 Day 20 lbs Challenge;* or *My 90 Day Journey To A Happier ME.*

"Changing your ways means also changing your diet. It's almost impossible to change your ways and not change your intake. Be it food and information (news, media, peoples' opinions, etc.)" – G-Anthony Moore facebook

Always be on Alert…

Think of every possible scenario, what are some of the things that can get in the way of you accomplishing your goals? I say "get in your way" because the only thing that can stop you is YOU. There will be detours; just be prepared to take an alternate route. Eliminate the chances of self-sabotage by realistically evaluating the start and finish points of each goal. My biggest obstacle is procrastination; although I work better under pressure, I tend to forget the fact that time waits for no one. So TAKE ACTION!

"If you want to live a happy life, tie it to a goal, not to people or things." - Albert Einstein

"You can't just be a recipient of a blessing; you have to do something to make it happen." - Bishop T.D. Jakes

"They always say time changes things, but you actually have to change them yourself." - Andy Warhol

For some of us, it takes having another human being come into our lives for us to realize our full potential. A good mate will inspire and encourage you to elevate and evolve.

I know a few of us have heard or said this before "I'm not ready for a relationship, it's not you… It's me." I've heard and said the same statement a time or two. When it came from me, I'm not going to lie; it was an excuse for me to get out of an unwanted situation. I felt like I was missing out on something, and in my mind, that person wasn't an ideal fit for me. As if Karma came to pay me back, I later heard the same statement from whom I thought at the moment was "the one." His excuse? He was working on himself and his career. Understandable, nothing is sexier to me than a man that's ambitious, but a lot of us have this backwards. Some people come into your life to add to you, not to take away from your progress. This Me Me Me mentality doesn't work for everyone and might lead to you losing out on a great person.

I like to believe that there are still people around that believe in what our parents and grandparents believed in, the concept of through thick and thin. I call these people "Builders" -- the men and women that don't mind working with the unfinished package; instead they work with you to build the total package. Making an investment in your future whether it includes them or not. For some of us it's hard to allow someone else to make that kind of investment and even harder for us to step outside of ourselves and invest into another person without there being self-gain. That's where compromise comes into play, a term that seems nonexistent nowadays -- Stepping outside of yourself to meet someone halfway. I know what you're thinking, "Here she goes again with this meeting halfway crap!" I have this funny belief that if everyone were to try to focus on their partners' happiness, actually taking the passage *"do unto others as you would have them do onto you,"* there would be fewer issues in relationships. I don't feel as though a person has to ask me to do something for me to act on it. If I feel you and our relationship is worth it, I will do anything in my power to make it work

IMPROVEMENT TIPS: Create a Vision Board -- Photographs, magazine, newspaper clippings, quotes and affirmations -- be creative with your vision board. There are also some sites that help you create vision boards and track your progress online, so that's another option. Try to look at your vision board at least once daily.

* If it takes you surrounding yourself with people and things that symbolize the things you want in life -- do just that -- make your own reality.

"People have been taught and believe that if they make a lot of money and find the right mate that they will be happy...but they got the equation wrong...the equation is...if you are happy, you will be successful and find the right mate. Happiness isn't the goal, its where you start from." - Juan William Jackson facebook

"Don't try to look for or find "the one." Be "the one" and you will attract it. - David Daudi Hicks facebook

"Most people are 'ready for love' on their schedule and that's why they miss it. They either rush in too early, or realize it is too late. Few are prepared for it when it crosses their path." - Jullian Goodin facebook

THE EXAMINATION

No this isn't a medical examination; this is where you pretend you are your own psychologist and you perform a self-evaluation. Here are some questions that will help you make a self-assessment. **This will be more effective if you write your answers down.*

Let's Analyze

1. Am I happy? If not, what's keeping me from being happy?

2. What have I accomplished thus far in life?

3. What part of my life do I love the best?

4. How well do I handle disappointment?

5. What are my insecurities?

6. What are the causes of these insecurities?

7. What are my general pet-peeves? *List as many as possible*

8. What am I grateful for?

9. What are my talents? How can I use my talents to better my life or someone else's?

10. Do I have realistic goals and visions?

11. What's missing from my life right now?

12. Am I an honest person?

13. What do I need to change about myself?

14. What's next for me?

15. What am I ashamed of? What's my greatest regret?

16. Where do I go wrong in relationships?

17. Do I care what others think about me?

18. Am I satisfied with my appearance?

19. Am I confident enough?

20. Am I settling for mediocrity?

21. Am I dwelling in the past?

22. Do I surround myself with positive people?

23. Do I love myself?

24. Aside from self, what and who do I love?

25. What personal barriers in my life do I have to overcome?

26. What are some of the things my past mates complained about? *Make a list of some of the complaints... If two or more complaints match up when comparing, there lies a fault you might want to work on.*

27. What makes me feel secure? What makes me feel insecure?

28. What am I most afraid of?

29. Describe yourself using 30 words or less.

30. What am I grateful for?

31. On the scale of 1-10; 10 being the highest, how would you rank the importance of these factors in your life?

______ Health

______ Money

______ Love

______ Happiness

______ Fame

______ Sex

The key to understanding a problem is first recognizing the issue. Pinpointing what's wrong and knowing where your weaknesses are helps you to strengthen these areas.

Ctrl

5 stages to Discovering, Dissolving & Evolving

Some may consider me as the violent type. My idea of a great first date is going to the gun range. There is something so empowering and relaxing about holding a gun, it's a huge turn on for me and a way for me to blow off some steam when I'm feeling stressed out. So it's only fitting I use a gun metaphor to illustrate my next thought.

What's your caliber?

As for me, I like to think of myself as either a 45ACP (Automatic Colt Pistol) or a Desert Eagle. My recoil (kick-back) may be a forceful thrust, but if and when handled by the right person, I deliver a mean and powerful blow. I'm what most people would consider untamable, and for the most part I would agree with that perception. I used to think of myself as a wild stallion, no man can hold me down, until someone came along and broke me. Broke, not in the literal sense of being broken or hurt, but in the context of breaking in a horse to train or make ride-able.

Everyone has characteristics in their personality that can be considered unchangeable or unmanageable; sometimes it takes the right person to come along and tame, handle, help you change or pinpoint that negative quality -- and then there are cases where you have to be the one that acknowledges and corrects those faults on your own. Humans are creatures of habit, so you may be very hesitant to change at first, but with change come progress, so it is important that you learn to stay open to modifications.

Sometimes it's not the people you choose to date that are the problem -- the main issue may be an underlying issue. Take notes or try to recollect some of the bad things others point out about you. We acknowledge and feed off of compliments. When someone compliments you on the way you're wearing your hair or makeup, what are the ramifications of these compliments? As a result of hearing positive criticism, we repeat the same action in hopes of more praise. As long as someone is not intentionally trying to cut you down, take notice of your negative feedback. This works with fortune 500 companies → "Give us your feedback, what can we do to *improve* your buying experience?" ← The key word here is ***"improve."***

DO NOT EMBRACE THESE FLAWS -- I often hear people say, "well, you have to accept me with all of my flaws." That's all crap to me. There is a huge difference between personal flaws and character flaws. Your pores being huge, fingers crooked or your thighs too big are personal flaws -- some of which cannot be controlled. A character flaw, on the other hand, affects your actions and motives. Being too possessive, extremely impatient, or very argumentative are traits that can be worked on in order to "improve" self.

TRY THIS:

Pinpoint your flaws, and then number them from worst to most manageable. This will help you find the correct approach to dissolving them.

Realize→ Analyze→ Improve→ Conquer→ Stabilize

REALIZE

I stated this before -- as with any other problems or addictions, the first step is to realize you do have a problem. You can't fix the problem if you are not honest and open enough to recognize a problem does exist. A flaw or fault is a vulnerability; eliminate a weakness by facing it head on. Think about the similarities between the type of people you date and the demise of your last 3 relationships. In all three circumstances, can you pinpoint your specific faults?

Set some time aside to truly evaluate your past relationships.

ANALYZE

Is there a common trait or habit all 3 past mates criticized or made remarks on? Are you *Judgmental? Too quick to assume? Selfish? Needy?* [One of my personal mistakes in relationships is disclosing every detail of encounters involving the opposite sex; from guys making passes at me to my past sexual relations. I later realized most guys are not concerned with the men that came before them or the men that are trying to come after them. Their only concern is where they stand with you... now.]

If you can't pinpoint your flaws, ask a couple of your close friends that have gotten the opportunity to observe you in a relationship what they feel are your relationship flaws. *This is one of the more effective ways of identifying your errors.*

SIDENOTE: Don't take their feedback too personal. Yes, some of the things they mention will rub you the wrong way, but think of it as constructive criticism.

Let's say jealousy is the cause of your failed relationships. Start off by asking three simple questions: When? Why? and What? When do these feelings arise? Why am I jealous over this? What actions follow this emotion and what are the consequences attached to such actions? The key is to identify and own up to your mistakes -- *"the truth shall set you free" - John 8:32*

IMPROVE

You have to work on your flaws and stop looking for someone to accept you as you are. Instead make every attempt to grow into a better you.

- Make notes and keep track of when these emotions or urges occur. Keeping track of your thoughts and feelings create awareness. Knowing when this emotion occurs will help you suppress and manage your behavior.

- Write down the characteristics of this flaw

  Ex: *Jealousy* is a form of fear, anger and being possessive, this emotion is often mistaken for love -- love is not angry nor does it cause fear.

- After writing down the characteristics, think about the most recent incident you had involving this flaw, how could you have handled the situation differently? Writing down alternative behaviors to your habit helps you envision positive results. Envisioning is the first step to putting things into action.

- Now, list each flaw and the specific plan of action(s) you will utilize to overcome those flaws. Writing your action plan down is one way to make things concrete and stick.

Example: *Claudia's* Faults

1. I assume too much

Resolution→ I must ask questions instead of placing blame.

2. I tend to tune people out when they are talking to me

Resolution→ I have to work on my listening skills.

CONQUER

Find ways to solve, mask or alienate these problems.

- **Fake It Till You Eliminate It!** I am not a fan of people putting on a façade, but in this situation, faking it is a necessary evil. Doing the complete opposite of an unhealthy habit can be a resolution. I'm going to use jealousy as an example again. If you put up a non-jealous front for long enough, not only does it mask your real emotions -- after a while the act can become a reality.

- **Create a positive action trigger:** A positive action trigger in this instance is something that will serve to invoke progressive emotion.

- **Think Back:** When jealous, try to think back to a happier moment between you and that person. Revisiting a past feeling of enjoyment or happiness can help subdue your current emotion. This will also help you condition, control and replace your negative thoughts and actions with positive ones.

- **Press Fast Forward:** Mentally fast forward and step outside of yourself and look at the situation from a third person point of view. Try to see the end result before it occurs. This gives you the ability and option to change the outcome.

STABILIZE

This is the most important of the 5 steps because if the issue or issues are not stabilized or terminated altogether, then the probability of regression is inevitable. *Ways to maintain your result:* Go back and read what you've written -- reviewing helps to clarify and put things in perspective. Where you are now versus where you were then -- this is a great affirmation technique.

- **Make it public:** Tell your family and friends about your decision to break your bad habit. Ask them to call you out on it if you backtrack. Having a good support system is always an added advantage when trying to overcome an obstacle.

- **Keep a current journal:** Use affirmations, inspirational quotes, self-help books, and meditation to uplift yourself. This will help you maintain your balance.

- **Practice healthy thinking:** Remember you are your thoughts.

- **Use positive self reinforcement**: Bad habits cannot disappear overnight, so don't put too much pressure on yourself, just remember to practice alternative actions and reward yourself when you do good.

The Boomerang Effect

Whatever you project into the universe; the universe has a way of sending it back to you, you've heard this theory said in many ways from various sources— to me— the universe represents Gods' mailing address. Whatever you write/send out to him— HE replies to directly, there is no forwarding address. The same thing goes for relationships, whatever you put into a relationship; you receive back in some way shape or form. Now there are some exceptions to every rule. There are some humans that are just not capable of being in healthy relationships for one reason or another, so no matter what one partner does to salvage the relationship, it just won't work. Both parties have to make an effort to make things work.

We go through so many phases in our romantic cycle. Lonely → Wanting Love → but finding Bullshit → Single by choice or circumstances → Something real hits us but we're too blind or hurt to recognize it → but if you're one of the smart and lucky ones, you stop wanting and looking, stop accepting the bullshit and voila! The universe sends you exactly what you *need.*

The key to finding something new or real is to get rid of all your preconceived ideas and notions, let go of the past and live in the *now*. Focus your energy on what you *need* right *now,* send out positive and you will receive the positive. For every action there's an equal or greater reaction and whatever we project, the universe will find a way to set it in motion. It's like reciprocation, when someone gives you or does something with you in mind, you feel compelled to return that gesture; this is how the universe works.

"Everything is energy and that's all there is to it. Match the frequency of the reality you want and you cannot help but get that reality. It can be no other way. This is not philosophy. This is physics." - Darryl Anka - a.k.a. Bashar

OPEN DOOR

It is said that *when one door closes another door opens*, the key to having the right door open up for you is visualizing yourself on the other side of the threshold. DO NOT UNDERESTIMATE THE POWER OF THOUGHT. Think of everything you want, need and expect; new house, new career, starting a new business, a good husband/wife, kids etc. When I say visualize, I mean actually taking time out to picture it in your mind. You should know the color of your door, what the doorknob looks like, even how many steps it took for you to reach your door. What type of door are you visualizing? Is it a sliding door? Maybe it's a swinging door? Visualize any door but a rotating one, unless you're the type that likes going in circles. Be very specific in your choosing. I chose a solid mahogany wood-framed glass door with a modern matte chrome doorknob. I chose a glass door because I like to see what my future looks like as I approach it…Solid wood frame signifies security and balance. See how specific I was on the type of door and the reason I chose it?

To help you visualize, do an online search for different types of doors, and choose one to your liking. After choosing the door to your future, find a way to keep that visualization in your forethought. Draw or paint it on paper or on canvas. Frame it and hang it on a wall. You can even save it as your desktop's screen saver or your smart phone's wall paper. Place it wherever, as long as it enables you to see yourself on the other side of your door. Once you are on the other side, lock the door and place the key in a safe place. In some instances it's probably best you throw the key away, altogether.

"The first person that we oftentimes let down is ourselves. It isn't our parents or children. We feel ashamed because of the time we wasted, decisions we made but didn't keep or never made, promises we broke to ourselves, or the dreams and desires that were aborted. There is no sense in regretting what hasn't happened. You can't go backwards. So stop allowing what you have done or haven't done stop you." – Pastor Michael Smith via Jullian Goodin facebook

Look closely at the present you are constructing; it should look like the future you are dreaming of. – Alice Walker

Let your *Talents* define your *Purpose*

My girlfriend Cathy called me to vent one day…She started going on about the father of her child always sitting around playing video games and going online to look at porn instead of him helping her with their 6 month old daughter. She felt she was being taken for granted and needed to find something else to do aside from the baby and having to watch the "big baby," (the father of her child). I gave her a dry answer to her problem, "Well then, find something to do." She seemed disappointed in my answer, and went on to say "I wish I had a talent like you do." I told her "everyone has a God-given talent; you just have to tap into it or figure out what it is." She stayed silent on the phone and then replied, "Well, how do I do that?"

EVERYONE HAS A TALENT, it's just that sometimes some of us pay no attention to it because it comes so naturally. A natural given gift is a talent; painting, writing even being a good listener is a talent. I will give you some helpful keys and questions that will help you tap into some of these talents.

- The first thing is finding a place to isolate yourself for a few hours or maybe a day or two; solitude and taking time out from the world helps ideas flow openly and helps you stay acquainted with your inner-self. While a man should always make time for his woman, a woman should always take time out for herself.

"Solitude, says the moon shell. Every person, especially every woman should be alone sometimes during the year, some part of each week and each day." – Anne Marrow

- You have to keep an open mind, get out of your comfort zone and absorb and try new things.
- Get rid of excuses and create ways to motivate yourself; self-motivation is the best motivation.
- Take notes of other people's talents. Some of us have those "Awww I always wanted to do that" moments. Stop awww-

ing and just do it! Just because someone else did it first doesn't mean you can't do it better.

- Find a way to capitalize on your talent; what are some ways you or someone else can benefit from your talent?
- Figure out what your strengths are and work on making them stronger.
- Do something for the first time!
- Make a list of all of your desires.

1. What compels you? What inspires you?

2. What comes easy to you?

3. What are some of the things you do out of obligation? People don't realize that some of the things we do daily can be considered a talent. Like cooking, just because it's considered a necessity doesn't mean it isn't a talent.

4. What do people compliment you on? Do people come over to your place and compliment you on your furnishings? Or maybe it's your overall sense of style?

5. What do you love doing? Do you get a kick out of fixing your friends up with each other? There are ways to capitalize on this talent, like throwing a dating mixer once a month. You are now creating a service; charge a nominal fee to attend your mixers.

6. Are you a good listener? Maybe you're a great problem solver? Well, capitalize on that. Start a website doing just that, or you can become a mentor. This is a great way to use your talents to help others.

7. What did you enjoy doing as a child? When I started writing this book, one of my girlfriends came over and while chatting she stated this, "Girl, I remember back in eighth grade when you tried writing that book, your handwriting was horrible!" A lot of the things we do as kids although we sometimes grow

out of it or suppress the desires, these things can very well be your calling, so revisit your inner child.

- Lastly, stay positive, and don't get so caught up in the term *"talent."* Just ....relax, clear your mind, and the rest will follow.

"Make the most of yourself by fanning the tiny, inner sparks of possibility into flames of achievements." - Golda Meir

Turning your I *NEVERs* ***into your*** *BUCKET LIST*

If you're like most people I know, you've had moments when you've seen someone do or try something and you say to yourself, "Wow, I wish I was brave enough to do that!" Creating a Bucket List helps you conquer your "I wish I could do that" moments. It's a way to turn your "I never" into "I will." A bucket list is a list of things you would like to do before hitting the bucket...Before you drop dead in other words. Let me rephrase that completely. A "Bucket List" is a list of *purposeful*, *meaningful* and somewhat challenging things, events, and places you compile and attempt to see, experience and accomplish before departing from this world—not to be mistaken for a "To Do" list; which is a list of daily or weekly activities or tasks you wish to complete. Having a bucket list serves the purpose of helping you create or build a compelling life story, it assists you with conquering fears and enables you to live your life to the fullest; experiencing things you never experienced, going places you've never been and doing things you never thought you would ever do.

Let's get you started with your bucket list -- one way to make things easier is to break your list into categories. You can choose to prioritize the things on your list in order of importance or you can fill in the sample list I compiled.

LEARN SOMETHING NEW - learning a new language, paint,

fly a plane, sword fight, singing etc.

____

____

TRAVEL - Tour Europe, see the 7 wonders of the world, sail the world, etc.

SPECIAL INTEREST - Run a marathon; ride on a hot air balloon, kayak, etc.

HUMANE - Start a charity, fundraiser, adopt a pet, shave off hair and donate it to *Locks of Love*, etc.

SENTIMENTAL - Make a family tree, start a family heirloom, write a memoir, etc.

SUCCESS - Start a business; purchase your first home, get that degree, etc.

LOVE - Fall head over heels in love, make love in the rain, start a family, etc.

RANDOM - Build a tree house, eat Moroccan food for a month straight, grant your own 3 wishes, etc.

SIDENOTE: Don't be afraid to have others make suggestions for your list.

"Twenty years from now you will be more disappointed by the things that you didn't do than by the ones you did do. So throw off the bowlines. Sail away from the safe harbor. Catch the trade winds in your sails. Explore. Dream. Discover." - Mark Twain

Esc

The ALPHA Woman

Society is ever so changing and evolving and with it is the roles women play. Women no longer only have the option to be submissive stay-at-home wives. With personalized Wonder Woman suits in their car trunks, they juggle education, careers, a love life, social events and some choose to add motherhood into the equation. *The unconventional woman is the new conventional lady.*

I refer to these new-age women as Polymaths or Renaissance Women. This is derived from the late Leonardo Da Vinci's drawing during the Renaissance called The Vitruvian Man which depicts the measure of a man in proportions. Having broad knowledge, being educated, proficient, self-sufficient, and well accomplished makes you a Renaissance woman.

I've witnessed a childhood friend of mine go from Alpha-woman to a subservient "House-Girlfriend." I use the term "House-Girlfriend" because she's doing everything a house-wife does without the title or a ring.

Camille possessed all the traits of an Alpha-woman: confident, intelligent, and attractive; quite simply…a man eater. She fell in love through an online relationship, a few months later they were living together, and she found herself being the only breadwinner in the relationship. This started putting strains on the relationship, and even after she would make threats to end things if he didn't get it together, she would re-nig and allows him to stay in her life without making any of the changes or attempts to fix the issues. Eventually, the love wore off, but Camille stayed in the relationship because of the fear of starting over again -- the fear of losing the time she invested into her man and the relationship.

When in relationships, some of us get comfortable with being comfortable. In Camille's case, I don't see anything comfortable about it. I had to make Camille understand that a man is no longer your man if you have to be the one to put food on the table, make sure he's clothed and supply a roof over his head. He is your child -- a man-child.

It's baffling how women of power are feeling the need to settle for second rate versions of men. For a relationship to work, both partners have to work towards a goal. As cliché as that sounds, it is the truth. It's alright to be submissive for the "right" man, but don't lose yourself doing too much for a man and not enough for yourself.

"The only reason I do for you is because I know and see you do for yourself." - @KillHershey twitter

Falling in love has a way of breaking down your barriers and rebuilding your foundation, but balance is everything. Love doesn't pay the bills, and just because you love someone doesn't mean you're meant for each other. If a man doesn't show consistency or the willingness to improve, it's time to kick him to the curb. Don't let the fear of starting over paralyze you. There are so many facets to a woman and the ability to adapt to any circumstance is one of our biggest super powers, you shouldn't have to settle.

"Men, understand, communicate, and demonstrate that her total sacrifice is not in vain. Both parties are in at the same level of investment, risk, and vulnerability. You won't see the full investment if she feels that you're not fully vested. She has to believe that there is no one in your past or future that can compare." - Pastor Michael T. Smith facebook

"Usually, not always, when a woman has to give a man an ultimatum. It's because she got with a man that wasn't ready to be in a relationship. A man that's READY will paint the picture that it's going somewhere. A man that's not will paint a fantasy. "I could see us" is NOT "I'm planning for us." A plan has things a woman can SEE. I could see myself on the moon...doesn't mean I'm planning a trip." - Jullian Goodin facebook

What new age *Hoes* can learn from *Whores* that made history

Reality TV shows, movies, social networks, club venues, everywhere you go -- it seems you can't get away from the glorified gold-diggers and hoes. These women publicize the fact that they are looking to be saved by a wealthy man. These glorified hoes blatantly make material demands and spectacles of themselves in the public eye.

From the times of the Bible, we hear of women that aided in the progress or the destruction of men. Delilah aided in the demise and downfall of Samson, and in Europe courtesans were said to have political influence on people of the courts. In the Geisha community of Japan, a woman is typically trained for a few years in various crafts and trades before being able to wear the title of a Geisha.

In a time where political and social lives were often mixed, Courtesans were high-class prostitutes that only serviced the men of the courts (i.e. Kings, Dukes, etc.). These Courtesans were intelligent and were said to be skilled and educated in politics and entertainment for the purpose of being novelties. Aside from sex, they were often called upon to showcase their many skills and artistic talents to members of the court. One of the most famous courtesans was Madame De Pompadour. Madame De Pompadour was known for her impressive personality and was notorious for being the official chief mistress to King Louis XV of France. Monica Lewinsky can be considered the modern-day equivalent to Madame De Pompadour.

Anne Boleyn was the mistress of Henry the VIII of England. Although Anne was not considered beautiful, she managed to win favor from King Henry through her outspokenness and willful spirit. Anne was said to have many talents; musician, composer, writer, singer, dancer and embroiderer. Her intelligence and various talents were what fascinated King Henry. Initially, the King bedded Anne's sister first, but Anne had her eyes on the crown. With her seductive charm and her compelling bedroom skills, she managed to persuade the king to divorce Catherine of Aragon so that she would be crowned the new queen of England. Her marriage to the king initiated a religious reformation.

These women used a mixture of seduction, intellect and talent to get what they wanted from men. What they all had in common aside from the mere fact that they had a vagina -- is vast knowledge and various skills, unlike a lot of new-age women that get by on looks and bedroom tactics alone. Having the ability to influence a man using more than just your pussy is a talent not many women possess. If you don't have it…acquire it. Pussy is power, but having a skillful mind and vagina gives you limitless powers.

GOLD-DIGGER	GOAL-MINER
• Gets him to buy red bottom shoes and bags with labels	• Gets him to clean, fix or boost her credit line
• Gets rent money	• Gets him to buy her property with her name on the deed
• Drives "His" car	• He pays off student loans, pays your tuition, buys your school books etc...
• All expense trips for your birthday	• Buys you stocks or bonds for your birthday

The chart above gives you a sense of what your frame of mind should be; if you're going to use a man for anything, have him invest in you, the material things in life don't last.

Reject your PUSSY

Reject Your Pussy and Accept your Vagina. A lot of you are staring at this section's title with a screw face because you're afraid of the term "Pussy"...Whether some of you admit it or not, some women use their pussy as a bargaining tool. "I'm going to give you some of this good-good and in exchange you have to pay my rent, pay my car note, take care of my utility bills, nails, hair, etc." He might as well put you on his monthly list of things to do and bills to pay. Yes, Pussy is a powerful thing, but living off your pussy is another thing.

While it may be true that a pretty face and a skillful "mouth" will allow you to get away with just about anything, ask yourself how long will that last? What else are you bringing to the table? What else do you posses as validation other than sex? A man can find that anywhere. I know what you're thinking..."He can't find my sex anywhere," but contrary to what you may believe, a man can find good sex and more, from a number of other women. Of course a man has to be able to supply more than just hard dick and bubble gum to keep a good woman around, and a good man knows this. A good man understands his obligations to a woman and won't require games and traps to get him to follow through. You want a man that comes equipped with more than just the standard options, so why wouldn't he want the same?

Value

Although a woman's vagina has value, it is not intended as a form of currency...You must value your vagina; I value my vagina so much so that I named it. I'm sure I'm not the first nor am I the only woman that has given their vagina a name, even before my first sexual experience I felt it was only right to name my vagina "Nana," unlike some of the egotistical names men choose for their penises, I went with a name that sounds subtle yet naughty at the same time. My vagina has a name because I respect her input on whom ***we*** decide to sleep with -- when, where and why? Nana has her own distinctive personality traits; she is loyal, devoted, expressive, aggressive and is very selective of whom she decides to spend her time with. *Know your vagina's value*. Some women think their pussy is worth millions, but in all actuality it isn't even worth Monopoly money. It's all about supply and demand, if you're giving up your goods to the wrong consumer, this will cause the value to depreciate. There's a competitive market out there in the dating world, so you have to make sure you put together a good marketing campaign and know who your target consumers are. Let me point out that I am not using the term consumer in the sense of a buyer/purchaser but in denotation of someone who consumes something—whether it is your time, energy or your affection of any sort.

Pinpointing your target consumer is the first step to putting together a good marketing campaign. You must determine what type of men you wish to attract; the caliber of men you choose will be what differentiates you from the rest of your competitors. Seeking someone that is financially stable and independent doesn't make you a gold-digger; it just shows that you want the best for yourself. But when seeking out the best, you have to be the best. Think of your vagina as a commodity; not in the sense of being bought and sold but being something of value, something useful. Every skill, talent and trade you possess, know and learn raises your value and your stocks.

Worth

If you had to put an actual price tag on your vagina what would you price it at? I'm willing to bet that your answer to that question is…"Priceless." Now, I know what's going through your mind -- it seems as though I just contradicted myself by asking you what price would you value your vagina at, right? But notice I was willing to bet that your definite answer would be "priceless," that's how positive I am that in terms of money—your worth cannot be calculated.

Learn the difference between earning and buying. Money and Pussy…what do these two things have in common? Men will do anything to "***earn***" them. They get more gratification from *earning* your attention and your vagina. PUT your PUSSY on PAUSE -- *P.P.P.* -- to better describe -- put him on an "Earning System" and reward him for his good deeds and good behavior, rather than just sleeping with a man in hopes of receiving gifts and favors.

"Have you ever noticed that Rolls Royce and Bentleys don't have commercials? Reason: They know the value of their products brings customers to them. Lesson: When you know your value, you don't have to beg people to like you, to be your mate, to spend time with you or love you. Everyone can't afford the luxury of your friendship." - Unknown – via Henock Aristide facebook

"When purchasing love, be sure to keep your receipt." - @KillHershey twitter

"Good twat twat -- good pussy isn't synonymous with loyal pussy. This is what we call misnomer -- a lie women tell themselves when a man stays with them...when he could be staying only because he doesn't have anywhere else to go." – Juan William Jackson facebook

"A man is not a financial plan" – *Kim Kiyosaki*

Taking Off Your Combat Boots

One of the hardest things I've had to deal with in relationships is my inability to take off my combat boots. I was always strapped and ready for war. I've always played the masculine role in relationships because of the fear of putting down my guard and letting someone completely in. I am very self-sufficient, so it's hard for me to allow a man to do anything for me. I don't want to risk having someone hang anything over my head. It's a pride thing, but because of my pride I was missing out on some of the real advantages of being in a relationship.

You can always count on your girlfriends to tell you the truth and point out some of the things you fail to notice. One day over lunch, my girlfriend Sal told me straight up, "Claudia, you really need to take off your combat boots, if not both then at least one. Let a man treat you how you should be treated."

I was suffering from what I call IWS, "Independent Woman Syndrome;" IWS has very similar symptoms to an ALPHA Woman -- waits for no man, walks to the beat of her own drum, etc. I felt as though I could do whatever a man could do; therefore, I took no crap from any man. Most of this temperament was built on the simple fact that I didn't want to be a burden to anyone. Subconsciously…I was burdening myself. Always trying to be the one to take care of myself and others left me stressed out and drained at times. One of the things I failed to realize at first is; *when locking others out I was also locking myself in.* One of the great things about being in a relationship is having someone there to help you untie the knots or carry some of your heavy loads.

A man wants and needs to be a man; he wants to know he's needed. A good man knows his obligations as a man and wants to earn the title of being "your man." While you may think you "got this" and you don't need his help, what you're really doing is conditioning that man to be unreliable; he'll always assume he's not needed which in time will be a hindrance on the relationship.

Having two of a pair is better than being or having one.

"*Teamwork makes the dream work.*"- John Maxwell

Men love self-sufficient women but are turned off by the women that feel the need to point out that they "don't need a man." A good man needs to feel he adds value to the relationship. Don't think of it as depending on a man. In a way he *needs you* to lean on him, a man wants to feel appreciated and accepted. Needing a man doesn't necessarily mean you need him financially. Lean on him for emotional support and stability.

As with everything else, moderation is crucial. There is a difference between needing someone and being needy. Everyone wants to feel needed, but what it all boils down to is two individuals *wanting* to be with and do things for each other equally. Two independent individuals make up a powerful force when both of them are *fully invested* in a *stable relationship* and have an understanding that having a good partner only enhances their lives.

The Bible says in Genesis 2:18-24 New International Version (NIV)

18 The Lord God said, "It is not good for the man to be alone. I will make a ***helper*** <u>suitable</u> for him.

19 Now the Lord God had formed out of the ground all the
wild animals and all the birds in the sky. He brought them to the
man to see what he would name them; and whatever the man
called each living creature, that was its name. 20 So the man gave
names to all the livestock, the birds in the sky and all the wild
animals.

But for Adam no suitable helper was found. 21 So the Lord
God caused the man to fall into a deep sleep; and while he was
sleeping, he took one of the man's ribs and then closed up the
place with flesh. 22 Then the Lord God made a woman from the
rib he had taken out of the man, and he brought her to the man.

23 The man said, "This is now bone of my bones and flesh of

my flesh; she shall be called 'woman,' for she was taken out of man."

24 *That is why a man leaves his father and mother and is united to his wife, and they become one flesh.*

Had to get religious on you for a bit but *real talk* -- Ultimately, a man wants a woman to serve as a partner not as a dependent or an independent. Being self-sufficient, but knowing how to balance our role as a woman is essential.

Only a beta man or a male equivalent of a battered woman would have been able to withstand the traits that I used to possess. Although independent, we secretly desire to be tamed. It's okay to be an independent woman, but it's all about finding that balance, and finding that balance only helps to intensify your existence. So try taking off one of your combat boots and allow a man to play his role.

Productivity - *Fake It to Equate It!*

I was over one of my girlfriend's condo, and both of us were lying on the couch bored with nothing to do when her phone rang. Before she picked up the phone, she asked me to start laughing. With a crazy look on my face I did what she had instructed me to do. As she pressed the answer button, she started laughing as well. She carried on the conversation with her suitor and told him how eventful her day was and quickly rushed him off the phone. When she hung up the phone I giggled and said, "You lying Bitch!" With a straight face she said dryly, "No man wants a woman that's always available."

While some women fake productivity, there are women out there that are more open than automatic doors. I know this because some of my suitors would ask me to come shoot the breeze with them or fly out to meet them here or there, and they would get upset or offended if I told them that I couldn't for one reason or another. These men are so accustomed to women jumping and dropping everything just for a chance to "shoot the breeze" with them. The women they deal with get gratification from being able to say they did this, that and the third with so and so.

So what's too open or too available and how do we balance it out? First off let me state, I am not an advocate of playing games but...*yes, there is a "but"*...faking productivity is almost always essential in the dating game. Never make it too easy for a man. Men always want what they can't have or can't understand.

Let me elaborate a bit (I'm always elaborating right? Lol) – well, when you are not busy doing you, you'll have too much time on your hands thinking about what he's doing or not doing. This leads to insecurities and insecurities repel. You'll start to nag about him not making enough time to be with you or that he's not making you a priority and so on and so on. When a man senses or knows you have too much free time, it conveys the message that he has to be the one to fill up that time. No man wants to have to spend that much time with a woman. A couple has to have their own lives outside of a relationship; you can't always expect him to come to your rescue when you're bored.

A woman with her own interests and life is too busy to have to worry about what a man is doing or not doing. Give the man time to miss you, it's much healthier, and if you have a good man, you won't have to remind him that you crave attention; he'll automatically know when to curb that craving.

Faking Productivity Tips:

- Try not to give too much details…a simple "I'm busy right now, let's talk later" or "I have prior plans for tonight" is sufficient.
- Keep small talk to a minimum, and know when to cut the conversation short.
- Pause for a few seconds before accepting a date -- this gives the impression that you are thinking it over or going through your schedule in your head.
- Don't always respond to text messages or emails too hastily -- a little delay never hurts.
- Lastly, almost always -- Be Busy. Which sounds better to you?

A. "I'm busy handling something right now, but I can free up some time to see you later this evening, are you free around 7pm?"

B. "Nothing, just chilling at home… looking for something to do."

(A.) Of course!

Key Words: "I can free up some time *TO SEE YOU*"

1. You put the ball in your court by setting up the time.
2. You made him feel significant, because not only did you allocate some of your time -- you also cleared out some of your schedule specifically for him.

"As women we waste too much time chasing men; stop being so concerned about what he's doing... who he's with and who he is doing. You fail to realize that you're only pushing men away! Here's a little advice: Men are like cats; when you chase them, they run. When you give them no attention, they want to rub against your leg and purr. You only live once, so don't waste time you can't get back because at the end of the day, that man is going to do WHOEVER and whatever he wants. Focus on yourself, find ways to occupy your time; go to school... HELL read a book! Just do you, any man worth chasing won't allow you to chase him." - Angel Thompson facebook

A woman will always be turned on by a man's drive, ambitions, and ability to balance himself to spend time with her. - @GOGETTA80 twitter

Backspace

What I'm Cooking, He's "Eating"

Now…This section's title can be taken two ways, and I mean for it to be taken both ways -- double entendre. Two things I'm very confident about are my skills in the kitchen and my skills in the bedroom. I won't elaborate on my bedroom skills because I'm sure every woman has her own personal tricks. They say *"the way to a man's heart is through his stomach"* ← This is not a myth, this is the utmost truth. (I'm sure the men will thank me for touching on this subject). There are way too many new-age women that lack traditional skills. Always remember one thing *"What you won't do, another woman will."*

Traditional male expectations of a woman include, but are not limited to: nurturing/raising children, managing the finances, emotional support, bed buddy (lover), cleaning, and -- of course cooking. Since the Stone Ages, men did the hunting and women did the gathering; this was considered doing and carrying our portion of the household load. Even as children we are introduced to the expectations and role of a woman through manufactured household and cooking toys. Should a woman have to cook for a man? My honest answer to this question would be— no -- and I'm pretty sure a lot of men won't list cooking as a requirement. But there is a contingency to my answer. While I feel a woman shouldn't have to do something she doesn't like doing just out of obligation, I do recognize my role as a woman. I understand it's hard to find time for cooking when you have to juggle a heavy workload, but when you do find that person you want to do things for; cooking will become more of a hobby than it is a chore. There's something sensual about cooking for someone you care for. I get a thrill out of coming up with different dishes and ways to garnish a meal. The look on his face is the kickoff to foreplay for me.

For some men, being with a woman that can cook serves as an emotional comfort. Men marry women they feel can take care of home and family -- nurturers. Yes, taking care of family entails cooking; cooking shows you have survival skills. A man wants to know that you can manage if times get hard and he's incapable of taking you out every week to eat. He needs to know you can do more than book reservations at a great restaurant.

TIPS:

- Try to duplicate a dish he enjoyed at a restaurant - This shows him that the meal was made completely with him in mind.
- *Cook and look good while doing it* - If your man is present while you're cooking, wear something naughty to keep him anticipating what's for dessert.
- *Get him to cook with you* - experimenting with different ingredients and recipes will titillate more than just his taste buds.
- *Have dinner somewhere other than the dinner table or in front of the TV* - doing something as simple as throwing a sheet and pillows on the floor and lighting a candle while trying a new Moroccan dish can add excitement -- show him how crafty and creative you can be.
- *Find enjoyment in catering to your man* - when you enjoy doing something it shows -- and everything tastes better when it's cooked with love. I know that sounds corny or cliché, but trust me -- it's the truth!

SIDENOTE: Make sure you're cooking for the *right* man, not every man deserves special privileges. With that being said, Ladies… If you don't know how to cook, take lessons. Google and YouTube are your best friends -- so find a few recipes and put your own twist on it. Feed him…and then "feed" him again. Thank me later ☺

"Some of these women want 'real men' to play the traditional role without the fussiness of having to hold up the traditional female role. Why can't we just accept the fact that times have changed... for all of us?" - Antonio Barnes facebook

What's on the Menu?

I've come across so many books and articles on how to catch a man, how to get a man to do what you want, and what men really want, etc. None of these books or articles focuses on what a woman has to bring to the table to get and keep a good man. We women make lists of what we want in a boyfriend/husband: he must have a good career, drive a certain car, be ambitious, driven, chivalric, etc. We seldom stop to think about what we have to offer the opposite sex.

A woman has to be able to serve more than just pussy on a platter. Yes, sex might entice a man or get him to pursue you, but with nothing else to offer, the right man will lose interest. What are you really bringing to the table?

Try this: Grab a pen, paper and a timer; answer these next few questions as honestly and quickly as you can. You only have one minute to do each of these exercises, so think fast. Jot down what you have to offer in a relationship.

What are you bringing to the table?

With looks aside…write down what specific attributes you think a man finds attractive about you.

Now, write down what specific <u>qualities</u> "you" find attractive about yourself.

In what areas are you lacking?

What are you not good at?

Compare all 5. Does your good outweigh your bad?

Would you date yourself?

When answering these questions, most of you will be biased.

It is not your fault. As humans, we are our own worst critics but we lack truthful self-verification; we seldom evaluate ourselves or our actions. Before getting into something new, try taking some time out to do things with yourself that you would normally do with someone you are dating. Pay close attention to the things that you are able to offer yourself; this will give you a clear indication of what you are capable of doing for another. Sometimes it takes dating yourself for a while for you to actually know what you can provide and what you want and need in a relationship, so don't be afraid to get into a *YOU-lationship.*

Now that you know what you have to offer in a relationship, take some time to write down what you want, expect and look for in a man. Try to put aside all of your unrealistic expectations, being selective is great, but try to remember; ***the basis or criteria by which you select is usually the same basis or criteria by which you will be selected.***

Don't get declined; know what you have in your account before making a purchase. - @Kill Hershey twitter

"The foundation of a solid relationship, first starts with being a whole single person. Your mindset should change from "Who is going to complete me?" to "Who can I add to?" You want someone that when you hook up with them, the two of you together SPRING forward. You're not correcting past issues from mom and dad's relationship or old boyfriend/girlfriend issues. Now you're a commodity. No one's trying to pay your bills, build the self-esteem, etc. You're whole. So to be in your life, they better be bringing something EXTRA to the table...not just what's needed. What's needed has already been taken care of— by you." - Jullian Goodin facebook

TERMS & CONDITIONS: Reading the Fine Print

However you start off a relationship or whatever you allow a man to do or get away with in the beginning sets the tone of the entire relationship. It is important to voice your like and dislikes from the very beginning. This protects you from any liabilities or disappointments. A lot of women complain about their man not taking them out enough, but it dates back to the very beginning. He treated you to a couple dates just to win you over, but after he got you, you allowed him to get comfortable and settled for just sitting at his place watching DVD rentals. You have to understand that in most men's minds taking you out a few times is sufficient. You'll get into an argument and tell him, "You don't take me out <u>anymore</u>" and he'll reply, "What do you mean? I've taken you out <u>before</u>!" not realizing the last time he took you out was a year or two ago.

So be sure to tell him up front what you like and dislike. Make statements like, "I enjoy going out on dates, a TV movie and home cooked meal is cool… but once in a while it's great to step out with someone I care for" or "I like receiving phone calls now and then because I love hearing your voice." Always follow your statements with somewhat of a compliment so that you don't come across as a nagger. It is also a good idea to affirm him on what he's doing right so that he stays in the routine, say something along the lines of, "I love the fact that you continue to do the things that got me to fall for you." Men work best with positive reminders instead of constant nagging.

Women have a habit of putting most of the blame on the man and not recognizing or accepting some of their own faults. It is always good to point out *some* of your own faults in the beginning and throughout the relationship, own up to your mistakes— think of it as a "Buyer Beware" clause. This will help you cut to the chase and save you some headaches— in most instances he will mirror you and disclose some of his own faults and spare you buyer's remorse. Everyone has faults, so be willing to negotiate the terms & conditions and try to compromise.

In case there are defects, (which in this case your defects are considered your faults) what are your warranties or remedies to solve them? Knowing how to protect yourself from being or becoming a liability is also important, so find or talk about ways to fix these flaws to better move forward.

"Women that embrace the bad as well as the good within themselves are sexy. Striving for self-mastery and being aware of self are compelling aphrodisiacs." - Coco Brown facebook

Assets vs. Liabilities

A few of my facebook friends were offended when I updated my status one day with this statement:

"I consider everyone in my life as either an ASSET or a LIABILITY; you are either aiding in my growth or setting me back."

They felt that I was treating people as material objects, but what I meant by that statement, although I think it is self-explanatory is this:

In any type of a relationship whether it be friendship, business, family or romantic, a person has to be willing to bring something to the table. One of the things *some* women fail to be is an asset when in relationships. They would rather swipe the credit cards than help balance the checkbook or keep his finances in order. Every relationship requires investments; whether long-term or short-term, both parties expect to see a gain or a return on their investment. Being an asset in a relationship means adding value to your partner, and the way you achieve this is by consistently going beyond what is expected of you.

Money issues are at the top of the list of reasons why relationships fail, and a large majority of men view women as financial risks instead of an investment, here are a few ways you can set yourself apart from the rest.

- **Support his dreams** - it's not enough to tell him "Baby, I believe in you"… help him with the leg work.

- **Set a monthly spending limit** - just as banks set daily spending limits on debit card transactions, it is a wise idea to set a monthly spending limit or allowance for you and your partner. Try practicing self-control and cut back on any unnecessary expenses, if one of you goes over the monthly allowance, the other should charge an overdraft fee.

Overdraft Fee: You and your significant other should come up with a penalty in case one of you goes over the spending limit. (Ex. No oral sex for 2 weeks).

- **Be a TEAM** - communicate before making final buying decisions. Big or small purchases -- you'll want to be on the same page when it comes to expenses-- same goes for any big decisions.

"And if a house be divided against itself the house cannot stand" - Mark 3:25, Bible

- **Have a Debt Plan** - Tackle your financial issues together; car loans, credit card payments, student loans, etc. In this economy, it's hard to stay clear of debt. If either one of you or maybe even both of you have debt, strategize and try to come up with a reasonable game plan to pay off those debts.

Tip 1: Start a joint "Debt Clearing" account together, transfer a designated amount every two weeks from your paychecks into that account, and pay off your loans in installments.

RELATIONSHIP **SIDENOTE**: Always remember, his money is NOT your money and vice versa. Always keep a separate account unless he puts a "ring on it."

MARRIED **SIDENOTE**: Make sure you have an *umbrella account* before doing this, every woman must have one; always be prepared for those rainy days…you never know what can happen.

Tip 2: Google - **F**air **C**redit **R**eport **A**ct. Contact all 3 credit bureaus, and order a copy of your credit reports. The FCRA states that any negative debts going back 7 years or more (10 years for bankruptcy) must be deleted from your credit report.

**You can find the FCRA summary of rights at:* Equifax.com

- **Be A Problem Solver** - Be a thinker - two heads work better than one, take the initiative; be that person that helps him put the pieces of the puzzle together.

- **Make. Money. Matter.** - Nothing feels better than having your money work for you; think of ways to maximize and create residual income.

- Talk to your partner about investing in stocks and bonds together.

- You can start an online shopping site *together*.

- If you are going out of town for a long period of time and your home or apartment is in a prime location, try renting it out as a vacation rental for the dates you are away.

- Vending machines are also a good way to create residual income, make sure you place the machines in high traffic areas.

- **Educate yourself and Share your findings** – There are so many business self-help books out there, read up on ways to increase income and share your knowledge with your partner.

- **Grow Together** – Nurturing, encouraging and learning are key components in a healthy relationship. Doing new and different activities together deepens your bond. Find activities neither of you have ever tried -- learning a new language, kayaking, sky diving, etc. These activities are guaranteed to wake up all your senses -- and the fact that no one ever forgets their first times is an added on bonus.

- **Give Back** - Find a charity you and your partner can donate to, doing good deeds together bonds you -- and as an extra bonus…charity donations are tax write-offs.

Be his confidante, his advisor, his banker and his lady. Try to be a one-stop shop -- the total package. No need for him to shop around if he can find everything he needs under one roof.

*These are just a few ways to help upgrade your partner and relationship. As a result, you and your significant other will see an increase on your relationship investment return.

"You are a Corporation! Make sure the people in your life are assets and ***not*** *liabilities."- @TheKillerTruthz*
twitter

The Art of "Stroking" the Male Ego

"He's got a BIG EGO"-- Just like women want and love to feel like the only girl in the world, men want to be worshipped like kings. They say a dog is a man's best friend, I beg to differ...In actuality a man's penis is his best friend, his confidante and his loyal advisor. Learn to stroke both his ego and his best-friend, and you'll succeed at winning him over completely. Here are a few tips and ways to stroke a man's ego:

Compliment his thoughts and ideas to enter his mind - Men pride themselves on supposedly being the stronger and "smarter" of the human species, this is why we women are obliged to be tactical and far more skillful. Nothing strokes his ego more than flattering acknowledgements.

Learn to compliment him using *Only* ***your eyes*** - What looks can tell. Master a seductive gaze. Look him up and down attentively. The imagery that will run through his mind as he tries to read your thoughts is enough to make his "best friend" rise to the occasion. People underestimate the power of eye contact; making eye contact with your significant other speaks volumes and also makes for a deeper and stronger connection

Acknowledge his Achievements - Men measure their worth on different merits than women; MONEY - POWER - RESPECT and PUSSY -- four things that drive a man. It's all an ego thing. Give him sufficient praises when he reaches a goal or feat.

Show Genuine Gratitude - A man likes to know when and what he's doing right. Showing gratitude not only shows him you appreciate him but this will serve as affirmation and encourage him to do it more often.

Praise him on Specific traits he possesses - If your man is a great listener, tell him that. "Baby I love the fact that you're a great listener." Pointing out the specifics helps to embed this behavior.

Compliment him on his physical appearance as well as his sense of style all at the same time - "Damn, I love the way your shoulders look in that shirt." Letting him know you like the way something accentuates one of his physical attributes adds depth to your compliment.

Give him Positive Reinforcement. Positive reinforcement is the act of giving or doing something for someone to promote a behavior. If your man does something good for you, take him into the bedroom and give him a reason to do it again. ☺

"The same way compliments are a necessity to a woman. Noticing and complimenting a man is also a necessity. A woman's ears, generally, are filled with compliments from other men that her man should be providing. Men's ears are generally filled with comments and complaints from their woman." - Jullian Goodin facebook

"After "LOVE," there's no greater feeling than when a woman tells her dude words like "Babe, I believe in you," or "I know you can do it, Babe." She could have told him she wants planet Venus for her birthday...he'll probably find a way to get it for her. Nothing like when a woman strokes a man's ego. #DJM... #stickingmychestout lol" - Henock Aristide facebook

"I am that motivation, my ego strokes cause happy endings." - @KillHershey twitter

Plant Your Seeds and Thank Him for Watering Them

While others use their pussy to get a man to do what they want him to do, there are some of us that recognize it takes more than pussy power to keep a man around. Most men believe their word is law, so nagging or trying to throw hints generally fall on deaf ears. Subtle suggestions and subliminal persuasion is key when trying to get a man to do what you want him to do. Men are visual creatures. You must use words that will conjure up images when using subtle persuasion.

Example

Normal: Why don't you take me out anymore?

Subtle Imagery Persuasion:

You: "Remember that restaurant you took me to when we first started dating? You loved the steak and the dessert was great…do you remember me giving you a little more than dessert when we got home that night? ;)

Him: "I was just <u>thinking</u> about that, they did serve a great steak…we should go on Friday after work."

You**:** "Great <u>idea</u> baby, I can't wait!"

You and I both know he didn't just think about revisiting that restaurant, but you planting the seed there made him believe he came up with the whole idea. Another form of persuasion is mirroring, you can use a subtle style of mirroring to break down his defensive walls. Voice tone or body language is one of the main causes of why discussions or disagreements escalate into arguments or fights. You can use mirroring to diffuse a dispute so that you may properly work things out. For instance, you and your significant other start to have a phone disagreement, and you both decide to continue the discussion later in the evening when you arrive home. You arrive home later and find your mate in the living room watching TV. Don't attempt to jump right in and make your case, instead sit beside him on the couch and try starting the conversation with something like this: "How's the game going?" Pay close attention to his body language and mirror him. As human beings, we are more acceptive and receptive towards the familiar. So mimic him subtly, if your mate turns towards you to explain the game turn your body toward him also, if he leans in to you, do this as well. Doing this will unconsciously knock down his walls and build enough trust for him to open up and *calmly* talk things through.

SIDENOTE: Make sure you wait until after the game to bring up anything from the phone conversation. You should never get between a man and his sports…You've been warned.

Some of the terms you may want to use when trying to get through to your mate is the

Who. When. Where. What. How.

These words also have the ability to conjure up imagery. Putting a desire or want into a question format makes the man feel included as opposed to feeling pestered or forced.

Example

You: "Baby, I think we should go to that restaurant you brought me to when we first started dating, *how does that sound?*

*Another thing you should keep in mind is that men are not good at taking hints, so as that old saying goes "a closed mouth don't get fed;" sometimes you have to come right out and tell him what you want.

The 3 C's

One of the more frequent complaints I've gotten from male friends over the years is this, "My girl stopped doing the things she used to do in the beginning of our relationship." I also get this same complaint from women about their men. The difference is when I hear it from a man, it usually tells me he already has one foot out the door, his interest has shifted. One of the biggest mistakes couples make is getting way too comfortable. Yes I know being comfortable is one of the reasons people choose to get into relationships, but being too content and getting too comfortable are the worst enemies to a relationship.

Here's usually how it happens...You start a new relationship and breeze through the honeymoon stages of it. You're spending all your free time with each other, the constant and consistent texting and phone calls, lots of sex, you're cooking for him, even doing some if not all of his cleaning. Everything is peaches and cream, you've even failed to notice a lot of his imperfections and overlooked his faults and shortcomings, and I'm sure he failed to do the same. Let's visit the three awful C stages of how things fall apart.

CONTENT: is first up to bat. You guys are satisfied with the way things are. You're sitting on cloud 9... Everything is magical and perfect, he can do no wrong and you are on your best behavior.

COMFORTABLE: This is where you start to become too at ease. You start feeling like "he's going to accept me no matter what, "take me as I am," you say. Laziness and procrastination comes right along with being comfortable, you stop dressing up for him, and he stops trying to impress you. You go from having sex 8-10 times a week, now he's lucky if he gets it twice. You used to make his favorite dish, now you cook only when you feel up to it. You see where I'm going with this.

CIRCUMSTANCES: Last up to bat are the circumstances. As a result of getting too comfortable, uncertainties and insecurities start to build up and set in. You may start taking each other for granted, the thoughtful things he does for you or you do for him go unnoticed, and things start to fall apart. As humans, we are creatures of habit, so it's not a surprise when getting into a relationship we tend to stick to doing the same things and never graduate past stage one. Nor is it rare that we get so comfortable that we forget it takes more to "build" a healthy relationship, so we sometimes fail to do the things it took to get that person in order to keep them.

Watering Your Relationship Tree

Be *continuously consistent*, whatever you did from day one to get his attention, continue doing it. *Example:* Cooking, cleaning, blow jobs, etc. If you can't consistently continue doing something you did in the beginning; try not to start doing it at all. A definite yes or no is better than a possible maybe, so stop false advertising. (This message was brought to you by our sponsors: Men)

- **Acknowledge his flaws and accept it; a man is not a project or something you can fix or change.** You knew what you were getting into from the very beginning; some say men change after they get what they want from a woman; I think the signs were all there, you just chose to overlook them. You can't expect a man "to take you as you are" and not be willing to accept him "as he is." Creating double standards just complicates things. People change when they want depending on the circumstances; you may *inspire* a man to change for the better but you can never force him.

- **Confidence, Strength, Assertiveness**...anything opposite of needy... be that.

- **HAVE A LIFE OUTSIDE OF YOUR PARTNERS**, I can't stress this enough. If it's not something he/she disapproves of, keep doing what you were doing before you guys met -- some of those things were what made you stand out in the first place.

- **Be supportive**, men are like children; they need and require constant positive reinforcement.

- **Let him know he is appreciated**. Take notes of the good deeds he does for you, stop letting them go unregistered. He changes your tires, fixes your bathroom sink, etc. Make a mental note then write a handwritten note or card letting him know you appreciate the little things he does.

- **Live in the NOW** -- bury past arguments.

- **Accept the fact that people and situations change**. This is what's so beautiful about relationships, it's always evolving. Find a way to make it work for you.

- **Never Stop Growing!** Oftentimes, one person stops growing while the other partner goes through persistent growth. Being content and too comfortable stunts growth— life changes, relationships are ever so changing; learn to evolve and adapt; never inhibit your progression.

- **Don't forget about yourself**. If you can't maintain a healthy relationship with yourself, expect the negative results of that to trickle over into your romantic life.

- **Stay in shape**, if you're not in shape, get in shape. Take good care of yourself -- work out, eat healthy make sure you have good feminine hygiene; make regular gyno and doctor's visits. Men notice these things, treat "yourself" good and he'll gladly do the same.

- **Rock some jeans, a t-shirt, cap and sneakers and look good while doing it**. All material and superficial extras are not always necessary; a man loves when a woman is confident enough to pull off that laid-back look.

- **Pull a change-up**; reinvent yourself from time to time to stay current. Just doing the same old same old will only bore him— if you have to create an alter-ego…do it! Use imagery (your style) and numerous elements of your personality to keep him absorbed in you.

- **Be Happy!** I didn't say act…I said "BE" happy, happiness is contagious, he notices that twinkle in your eyes when you smile. If he's had a hard work week, use your energy, smile and laughter to cheer him up.

- **Get into what he's into or at least learn to fake it.** Sports, cars, collector's items, whatever else tickles his fancy. Women complain when a man gets so wrapped up in the TV watching sports that he forgets about spending quality time. Well, get him to explain the game to you; if you're part of his favorite pastime, it won't bother you so much.

- **LISTEN!** Finding a woman who listens is like finding a needle in a haystack. Learn to examine the situation + evaluate your thoughts as well as his words before you give your final verdict or *assumptions*. Even if you don't agree and know that whatever is coming out of his mouth is bullshit, just the simple fact that you took time out to listen helps subdue the situation.

- **Buy him something special.** You like gifts, well so does he. Buy him something useful, something he won't just put away in his closet.

SIDENOTE: Make sure you and your mate have mutual feelings for each other, I've had countless chats with male friends that complain about women they're 'just' sleeping with buying them gifts. I mentioned this before but let me reiterate -- Sex DOES NOT constitute a relationship. Some of these men find these gift gestures annoying and somewhat pathetic, so make sure you both see eye-to-eye before making a purchase. If you're unsure about where you stand…don't buy anything at all or just save the receipt.

- **Don't search for the negative** because chances are you will find them. Instead, focus on trying to CREATE the positive.

- **The 3 Positive C's** – and these are very important key factors in a healthy relationship. **COMMUNICATION, COMPROMISING** and **COMPLIMENTS**. You might wonder how compromising made it, considering the fact that the word compromise is usually used in the context of settling for less. Relationships are agreements. When entering into an agreement, you sometimes negotiate the terms before reaching or making any final decisions. Chances are, you won't agree to or accept everything that is listed in the contract, but keeping an open mind and learning to compromise will help balance out future issues.

- And last but certainly not least…**Give Him Lots of Blow Jobs!** I know a lot of women out there don't like or are not comfortable with giving a man oral sex, but we're in the 2000's honey, you may have gotten away with not doing it in the 90's, but you gotta get up-to-date with the program. Almost all men love to be pleasured orally, so learn to love giving it, if you need tips on how to do it, don't be too shy to watch a porn flick. Mark my words "more head equals less problems."

Bonus Tip: Set your alarm clock 10 to 15 minutes before his wake up time and give him a rooster of a wakeup call by going down on him. I guarantee waking him up in that manner will set the tone for the entire day, maybe even the week. *Cock-a-doodle-do!…You're Welcome.*

"A little relationship advice to my fellas, just remember guys— a relationship is like a small tree. You have to water it and take care of it daily, once you stop it will eventually die. You can't get comfortable, because being comfortable is a recipe for disaster. Women need daily reminders, stop assuming she knows she is beautiful -- you must remind her. If you know she loves to dance, then dance with her. Never stop showing her you appreciate her."

– Nathan Fragelus facebook

Cause and Effect

For every action there is a reaction -- I've been saying this throughout this book. Eventually, it will sink in. Certain things people do can cause you to react in an unjust manner. In relationships there are ups and downs; only the strongest survive. A lot of times we concentrate on who's at fault rather than ways to solve the issue. Instead of who's to blame, try asking yourself a few simple questions.

1. Am I correcting him/her for my benefit or for *our* benefit?

2. What are his/her needs and how can I meet them?

3. Am I being realistic?

4. Am I being too demanding?

5. Am I being ungrateful?

6. What was the cause of this argument?

7. How can I prevent this situation from escalating?

A lot of times you'll start to argue about one thing and fall into the trap of arguing about a hundred other non-factors. You can't always be in the right or win every battle, know when to be the bigger person and call a truce. There has to be a balance, when one partner is upset the other must try to find a way to diffuse the situation. You can say something like "You're so damn sexy when you're mad" to appease a conflict.

Sometimes arguments strain deeper and can't be appeased so easily. If this is the case, remember *shit happens*, so confront the situation and move on; cross that bridge together. Do not confront in anger, keep a calm and cool tone when speaking to each other and be sure to stop and really take time out to listen.

"James 1:19 New International Version (NIV) 19, My dear brothers and sisters, take note of this: Everyone should be quick to listen, slow to speak and slow to become angry."

RELATIONSHIP EVALUATION

1. What are your expectations when entering a relationship?

2. What tends to be your attitude when in a relationship?
Ex. A lot of people in relationships want to be single, but once single they miss being in a relationship.

3. What are some aspects of your character that can be changed to improve your current situation?
Ex. Communication, Understanding, Dependability, Judgment, etc.

4. In what ways have you changed in your relationship from your first date until now?

5. What are some important lessons you've learned from prior relationships?

6. What are the strongest areas in your relationship?

7. What are the weakest areas in your relationship?

8. Does spirituality play a part in your relationship?

9. What stage of the relationship cycle are you in now?
Courtship – It's only the beginning -- both partners are on their best behaviors→**Romance** - The honeymoon stage - passion, passion, and more passion→**Stable** - this is the ideal stage→**Refund** – This is not what I signed up for→**Limbo** - it's rocky, but things can go either way or we're taking a break to see where things go→**Dead End** – There's nowhere else to go but out.

10. What stage do you believe the relationship should be in?

11. What type of relationship are you in?
Ex. Sexual, Monogamous, Committed, One-sided, etc.

Knowing what type of relationship you're in puts things in perspective and prevents gray areas and in some cases… heartaches.

The Answers

Here are a few common topics and questions I've received over the months, some of which I've even asked myself at one point. I'm sure a lot of you can relate. I'm going to give you some very straightforward answers, so *excuse your feelings.*

"When is it an appropriate time to mention past relationship(s) to someone you just started seeing? Or should I not mention it at all?" - Berlandgie David

People often point out the common misconception that you should not talk about your ex with a new mate. I agree with this partly, while you probably shouldn't mention anything about your ex to someone of interest on your first few dates. I think at some point of getting to know each other, you can use your ex as a "what not to do to me" reference point, sort of like a "How to" Not Fuck Me Over tutorial. It's really a safety measure. If he is a good man and has your best intentions at heart, he will take heed and try his best not to make the same mistakes your last mate did.

As a disclaimer let me state -- this won't work for everyone, you have to be able to feel the person out. Some men and women can't handle the details of your past relationship(s). Do not voluntarily dispense details; when the time comes he/she will cue you in. When they do inquire about your dating history, try to answer directly to the question(s) being asked, and keep it very simple. Openness and being able to reveal some of your baggage to a potential mate is part of *accepting all of you.*

***"I'm happy in my current relationship, but I often wonder should there be more…* AM I MISSING OUT ON ANYTHING?" - Sonia Holms**

I've experienced brief moments of uncertainty when in a

committed relationship, and I'm sure I'm not alone. When in a relationship, you feel you're missing out on something and when single, you realize there's really nothing out there. When in a committed relationship, there's a great chance you will encounter men that are better looking, more educated, charming, caring, just plain better than your significant other, and there's an even greater chance he will encounter women that have a lot more to offer him than you do. That's why relationships are sacrifices, an ultimate test for both partners.

Yes, better will come along, but how long will they stay? People that cheat or leave a good person for a situation they "think" is better than their current situation are taking a big risk. Making permanent actions based on temporary feelings is never a good idea; the grass is not always greener on the other side. While there are better people out there for you and your mate, together you guys may be a better match.

"My girlfriend always nags me about the same thing -- even after I think we bedded the issue. How do I get her to leave past situations in the past?" - Mike Sinclair

Mike… get her to read this:

Finalizing an argument -- A lot of times arguments are just continuations of prior arguments, problems carried on from unresolved issues. It is important that you confront and work these issues when they occur; stop making your mate pay for the same thing over and over again. Once you talk about it … dead it. If he continues to be a repeat offender that's a whole other issue— when someone does something once, twice and so on, it might be because you didn't point out the problem the first time it occurred. When your mate does something you disapprove of, it is best you voice your disapproval in a calm yet firm voice, do not let it build up… build-ups lead to clogs and spills; neutralize the situation right away.

"My boyfriend will post photos of everything and everyone he cares about online but neglects to post any pictures of me… what does this mean, and how do I address the issue" - Chelsea White

One of the things people use social networks for is to show the world what they enjoy and care about -- daily activates, bragging, etc. I, for one, rarely believe that people are actually doing what they post they are doing unless they post pictures of them doing it. Too many posers out there acting as if they are living the lavish life when in all actuality they are just laying in bed posting whatever comes to mind. This is why I like the whole Instagram movement, rather than saying it… just show us.

Post My Picture, So I Know That It's Real

I'm trying to find the words to ease into this and let you down as easily as possible, Chelsea. Okay…Here it goes…If your significant other doesn't post pictures of ya'll, chances are you are not the only person he is seeing. Especially if he posts everything else in his life— there is also the probability that he is ashamed of you. Not necessarily ashamed of how you look; it's just some people like to keep up the whole bachelor façade.

If this bothers you, speak to your mate about it; let him know you want to feel included. If he can't give a legitimate response or solution for this, then it's time to evaluate the situation and your relationship.

SIDEBAR: There are some rare cases where a person won't post pictures of their significant other because they don't want others prying into their romantic life, but like I said…these are rare cases.

"WE DON'T BELIEVE YOU, YOU NEED MORE PICTURES!" @Kill Hershey twitter

"Ok, I've been seeing Sam for a little over a year… we enjoy each other's company, the sex is AMAZING and we do everything boyfriends and girlfriends do, but he will not agree to a title! He says he's not ready and is trying to get his life in order…how do I convince him to commit?" – Tonya Love

An orgasm does not equate to a relationship -- Some women mistake dating for a few months with an actual relationship, just because you're spending time with a man and he's giving you multiple orgasms doesn't mean he is *your* man. Dating is a few months process -- If you're going on a year or more, and there still isn't a title, chances are he will never make that commitment. Yeah, I know, people change and situations evolve, but without the title, you're just someone he's seeing until someone better comes along. You are only an option; not putting an official title on things only benefits him. He can see other women and when you're upset and hurt about the matter he can use this magical phrase → "We're not even together."

The only way you can get played is if you allow yourself to be part of the game. Unless you have a real conversation with a man about taking it to the next level, you are only an option. Spending time with a man does not equal a relationship or love, take back your power, give him an ultimatum -- become the choice instead of staying an option.

"I have always played the masculine or motherly role in every relationship I've been in. I understand I'm a strong woman, but I'm starting to get tired of paying for everything… so what gives?" - Brooke Charles

Yes, good men are very scarce, and it's like a battlefield out there, since it's three women for every one man— in some cases five to one. I'm noticing more and more women are becoming "sugar mommas." It's one thing to hold down your man and be that ride or die woman but having to pay a man to stick around is unacceptable.

This has become so much of a trend that there are actual dating websites dedicated to just that, helping men find women that will take care of them; he's a warm body in your bed and you're a convenience to him. There are a lot of role reversals in this generation, but women are going the extra mile to convince men to get into relationships with them. If we're paying and doing everything for a man what obligations is he left with? The sex? Honey, there are toys that will get the job done for less than you're paying him.

Always paying and letting someone take advantage of you is not a form of strength, rather a form of weakness. Although I'm somewhat old-fashioned when it comes to the mating and dating ritual, I do believe there are some occasions a woman should pay. Never on a first date—unless you're the one that asked him out and insisted on paying. I myself will pay for a date if he's the one that paid for our first few dates. I do this to show appreciation, not out of obligation. It's always a good look for a woman to offer to pay for the tip from time to time -- doing so gives you merits. Most men won't actually allow you to pay, but he'll find the gesture refreshing.

There is a huge difference between being a good woman by helping and holding your man down in his time of need versus knowingly paying a man's way. Settling down doesn't mean you have to settle.

"People have no idea what a man is. We know what a "male" is. You can point that out on a chart. But the Bible says that, "If a Man doesn't work. He doesn't eat...and we have so many women out there financing their sorry tails!!" - Pastor Michael T. Smith

"A guy that gets with a woman for what she can provide materially/externally treats her as such. As something that he will eventually get tired of, and something that depreciates over time. And now he's used up that woman's prime years. And like a parasite, that type of guy moves on to the next. But a Man that gets with a woman for what she can provide internally treats her as

such, too. Because he understands that over time she should become a better version of the woman she is now -- and becomes more valuable, to him, in his life. It's important to be able to discern between these types of guys. But even more important is discerning how men view you as a woman. So many women lead with showing butts and breasts, and then want the guy to get to know her internally. And most times he gets to know her internally. Just not in the way I'm talking about here." - Jullian Goodin facebook

"My girlfriend has a habit of always assuming I'm up to no good when I don't disclose full details. How do I put her mind at ease?" - Caleb Peterson

My "last" used to always tell me that I assume too much and that people that assume always make an "ass" of themselves. I tell him assurance is everything. I wouldn't have to assume if you didn't leave room for assumptions…too many gray areas are never good. As women, if we are left to question things or put the pieces together on our own, we will come up with the worst possible scenario. This is why people must learn not to do or say things that your partner will find hurtful or have to question.

I would tell you to ask yourself— "How would this affect you, if you were in her position?"—whenever you do something that would come across as disapproving -- but the truth of the matter is, not everyone is affected by the same things. What may not seem disrespectful or unnerving to you may be very hurtful to your partner. If you're with someone, you should have a feel of what would get under their skin. So the real question is not "How would you feel if the shoe was on the other foot?" The real question is simply, "Would my girlfriend be hurt by my actions?" Try to be forthcoming when she seems uncertain, have a clear line of communication and always leave an open floor for discussion.

"When you do your part to keep strife out of your relationships, you are honoring God." @JoelOsteen twitter

"I can't get my boyfriend to open up about what's been on his mind lately, he seems so distracted. Maybe I'm doing something wrong or could it be he's thinking about another woman?" - Natasha Bale

A man's silence has nothing to do with you; maybe he's dealing with a work matter. Just because he's caught up in his thoughts doesn't mean he is caught up with thoughts of another woman. Understand this… Men love their alone time, as simple as that may sound; some women treat it like rocket science. Watching the game, playing golf, ritual basketball on Sundays, whatever his pastime is…he needs that release— that time away from all his stress, problems and yes….you. Not that you are a problem or the cause of his stress, he just needs that time to refuel. So stop stressing yourself out so much -- go hang with some of your girlfriends, or take up a new hobby; once he's refueled you can hop right back into his passenger seat.

"My friends tell me the reason I can't keep a man is because I'm too clingy and needy… how do I keep from coming off as too needy?" - Samantha Jean

A lot of women suffer from emotional dependency and don't know it. Some women even display this trait in the early stages of dating, way before he has invested his feelings into you. A man can feel when a woman's happiness is dependent on him, and neediness will fend off a man. Most men want women that don't *need* them, they tend to run away from the two awful D's -- DEPENDENCY and DESPERATION. The best way to avoid being needy is to 1. Stay occupied with your own life. 2. Do your own thing; always remember you have your own likes and dislikes; your own thoughts and ideas, so when dating don't always go along with what he wants to do and don't be afraid to voice your opinions. 3. Avoid calling and texting him every chance you get, let him miss you. Seeking too much attention shows a lack of confidence -- remember with everything there is a balance, too much of anything is almost never a good thing.

"I've been seeing an awesome guy for a few months now... he wants to take things to the next level, but I'm afraid. The last guy I was with hurt me deeply, I am still working on putting myself back together. How do I tell the new guy all of this? - Tracy Paul

Good Guy Wrong Time

You are incapable of allowing a good man to treat you right because the wrong man broke your heart, shattered your mind frame and you weren't able to glue the pieces back together on your own. There is no magic pill to mend a broken heart and spirit; I will tell you this though, you can either be like Noah and do the building on your own which took him 120 years, or you can get a contractor and work out the floor plans, then do the building together. Try not to make this new guy pay for what your last boyfriend put you through. Everyone comes into your life for a reason. Look at it this way -- your last boyfriend served his purpose; his ill treatment made it easier for you to recognize what a great guy your new potential boyfriend is. All he did was make room for someone better to walk into your life. Let this new guy aid you in putting the pieces back together -- and keep the past where it belongs ...in the past.

"Build a sturdy bridge instead of just crossing one to get to the next." - @Kill Hershey twitter

"I sometimes seek advice from my boyfriend's male buddies; well...one in particular. He gives good insight, and we are building a friendship, but I don't want this to cause any issues between my guy and I. How do I keep it respectful, so that neither of them gets offended? - Sandy Porter

In all of my relationships, I've always made allies with the one of my mates' friends; this always helped me get my point across to him, and at times has helped me understand his mind frame during a disagreement. I've had instances where his friend would reveal more than what should have been revealed. This has always worked in my favor; an ally is that one friend your guy has that recognizes your worth and will at times remind your boyfriend of what he has. Although an ally is great to have, there is a very fine line, and you should always be careful not to cross it.

It all depends on who you are involved with because he can see this treaty as a threat and dismiss you and/or your ally. The fact that you're asking this question shows me that you already feel you may be doing something your boyfriend wouldn't approve of -- If you have to second-guess something when in a relationship— then chances are you shouldn't be doing it. Save yourself the headache… and respectfully cut ties with your guy's buddy. Let him know your reasoning -- I'm sure he'll understand.

Be Careful of the Double Agent - Not everyone is trustworthy, so be careful of double agents, some people will act like they have your best interest in mind but always remember at the end of the day…The ally is originally your mate's friend, not yours.

Another thing you should stay on alert for is the agent that has an interest in you. He may place thoughts into your head to ruin your relationship so that he himself can slide in.

Take all of this into account when dealing with an ally.

"I have yet to meet a man that wasn't a liar and a cheat… men are nothing but dogs. Why can't I find a good man? - Page Grant

All men are dogs? Is this a fact or common misconception? Let's really think about this…I am both a dog owner and a dog lover; when comparing men to dogs, yes it's safe to say they have very similar traits and behaviors. They follow you around, do tricks to get your attention and approval, but just like there are different breeds of dogs, there are different types of men. For example, you have your attack dogs; attack dogs are trained to attack on command or from receiving a certain look. In comparison, there are men that attack or pounce from just a simple glance from the opposite sex. I know some of you experienced going to a party or a crowded restaurant and attempting to make your way to the restroom -- if you're like me, you fix your eyes on the restroom sign just to not mistakenly give an overly thirsty man eye contact. By unfortunate fate, you take your eyes off your mark just for a second and BAM! Your eyes meet his eyes for 1.3 seconds and while you quickly try to undo your wrong, he grabs your hand and tries to sell you on a pitch. We've all been there, smh.

Domesticated dogs and good committed men are similar because when given unconditional love, they are extremely loyal. There is also a popular notion that dogs don't think, they simply behave and that men only think with their "other head," but putting all men in the same category would be like saying all women are gold-diggers. If all men are dogs, then it's all up to you to choose the right breed.

So whenever I hear a woman make the statement "all men are dogs," I can't help but think one thing -- maybe that woman is just not fit to be a dog trainer. A man will only do what you allow him to do. It takes **P**atience, **P**ersistence, and **P**ositive reinforcement to get a man to act right -- put the 3-P's to practice along with some occasional P* and you just might tame a wild dog.

"Men are not the enemy, but the fellow victims; the real enemy is women's denigration of themselves." - Betty Friedan, Women's Advocate

"Women are to blame for some of the ways these new school men act; yes you are to blame for his behavior. What happened our Queens? I am not saying a man has to be Prince Charming, but come on. If the guy can't even hold a real conversation without talking about sex, and how bad he wants to do you. If the man just wants to come over instead of asking you on a real date and you just met him. If the man approached you with one hand holding his pants and the other in his head, if the man can't even address you

by your name or miss, if the man doesn't know it's common courtesy to bring you flowers once in a while not for a specific occasion. If the man has no respect for his children's mothers, or barely talked about his kid. What in your right mind would make you think he's the right man for you? Let me guess...he got swag? Nowadays, women are willing to settle for anything for the sake of the unknown and society. As long as they are sexually satisfied, it doesn't matter what a man does, and most of the time they're not really truly satisfied because they are simply the side chic. I hate to break it down to you, before blaming men, before calling us dogs please take some time out and find the reason why you are attracting these types of men." - Nathan Fragelus facebook

"Okay ladies. I know I'm going to hurt some of your feelings, but you need to hear the real truth. You go out there and look for the "swag and sag" and you pick up the guy with 5 babies (that he sees once a month) from 4 baby mamas with no job and for some reason you think that you will be able to change him. You think that you are such a catch that he won't leave you. Then when he does leave you, you have the nerve to say "men are dogs" and deadbeats etc....Well the truth is that you knew what you were getting when you picked up that bum. That's only a small percentage of the men out there, but it seems that those are the ones that you are choosing. Whereas the clean cut, hardworking guy is considered boring and "gets no play." Whatever happened to the days when a woman wanted a man that can help to expand her mind? A man who will take her to a play or an Off-Broadway show instead of just the drive-in. To make a long story short, don't blame the bum you picked up, blame yourself for picking up the bum. IJS" - Steve Barrow facebook

Ctrl
Alt
Delete

Creating and setting boundaries from the GET-GO

SCENARIO 1: *You call him, but he doesn't answer. Less than a minute later, he hits you with a text that reads: "What's up? I was on the other line" or worse -- he updates his social network status.*

The new age man will give you the excuse that he doesn't like talking on the phone because of one reason or another. Chances are he really wasn't on the other line, he just didn't answer intentionally. A man that considers you a priority would've sent a more fitting text like "Hey, I saw that you called…I'm on a business call and will ***call*** you back as soon as I get off the line."

How to counteract this situation: You can do one of two things, (1) not answer any of his text messages, which will prompt him to call you if he in fact wants to communicate with you. When he does call, calmly express your disapproval; let him know that if you wanted to get a text back from him, you would've sent out the initial text instead of calling. Follow that statement up with giving him a compliment "I enjoy hearing your voice every so often." Or (2) you can send him a reply stating the same sentiments, but I do think option number (1) delivers more of a concrete message.

SIDENOTE: It takes more effort to send out a text than it does to pick up the phone and call someone— to articulate what you have to say and be done with that ←this should help make your case if he hits you with the "but it's easier to text" line.

SCENARIO 2: *You make plans to go on a date with a person of interest for* ***around*** *3pm, but three hours after 3pm you're still sitting at home waiting for him to pick you up.* First off, this is a clear indication that he doesn't respect your time. When he does call, tell him you are simply not feeling up to it and reschedule for another day.

How to pre-counteract to this situation: When setting up a date; in order to prevent let downs or your time being wasted, make sure to set a solid time. Do not leave anything up in the air or play it by ear. Avoid the word "*around*" this or that time, instead say "I'll see you at 7'oclock." This will give him the option to either push it back to a later time or confirm with an earlier one. When you both agree to a proper time, be sure to reiterate it to him and let him know that your time should not be wasted. *Ex.* "Okay, 7:00PM sounds good to me… if something comes up and you can't make it, please call or text so that I can make other plans for tonight."

This will increase his chances of showing up on time and will make him second guess canceling on you if something else does come up. Knowing that you have other options for the night will make him put in more effort because there's a great possibility he thinks those other options may include other suitors.

SIDENOTE: Do not lead him on to think you have no other option. If he does cancel on you and you have him on any of your social accounts, be sure not to update your account with any lonesome statuses. Men love a woman that doesn't need or count on them to have a good time.

SCENARIO 3: *You get the "What are you doing?" the "I was thinking about you." And even the "I miss you" text but never a follow through "I want to see you," "Let's do something tonight" or the "I'm coming to see you" text.* Let's face it… most men are horrible at fully expressing these sentiments; they lay a half-assed offer on the table and leave it up to us to close the deal. Don't take offense to this…in this case it is truly them and not you; a lot of this has to do with their fear of rejection. While it is true men have the balls…women do in fact make the rules, the "balls" are always in our court.

How to counteract this situation: The next time he sends you one of those "What are you doing today?" texts, help him out by hitting him back with a *"Why, are you trying to see me? Lol"* or a

"You want me to make room for you in my schedule? Lol" text; this helps seal the deal.

In order to achieve something healthy, you have to recognize and weed out the unhealthy fragments. Clear communication is very crucial to achieving this; you must not be afraid to vocalize your criterion. Here are a few DO's and DON'Ts to help nip out the bull crap from the get-go (the beginning).

- Remove the following words and phrases from your vocabulary: "Sure", "maybe", "that's fine", "ummm", "let's play it by ear", "you tell me", etc. These words and phrases leave too much room for error. Replace them with a simple YES or NO. If it makes things easier for you, make a list of things you will and won't tolerate.
- Do not agree to being on standby or drop whatever you are doing for a man -- being too available screams desperation.
- Do not negotiate your time; let your suitor know that you have better things to do than to play games.
- Do NOT delete, backspace or edit your standards, requirements, decisions, or however else you want to word it. Reneging on your statements or thoughts makes for a shaky ground, be very concrete; command your respect by standing your ground. I must stress— always make your points clear by being calm, cool and respectful with your statements. Men love strong and assertive women; not to be confused with being a bitch. Excuse my French.

"No one draws invisible lines, visible lines are made by boundaries of conversation" – Michael Hall

CHOOSING YOUR BATTLES

A married male friend of mine said something that had my mind boggling for days, he said "My wife knows I use these social networks to cheat, but what makes her different from other women is she knows how to pick and choose her battles." He went on to say," I take care of home, I'm a good husband and father…every man cheats, if you don't believe that, then you're probably one of the people that believes in Santa Claus. A man is going to be a man, but my wife has a choice, she can stay with (me) a man that cheats but is a good husband, great father and a provider. Or she can leave me and find another man that's going to cheat on her down the line also, but won't give the things I provide her with." His idea of a choice sounded more like an ultimatum to me, a catch 22... Damned if you do, damned if you don't.

More and more men are using these social networks to cheat, and as a result, more and more relationships are being ruined from just a click of the mouse. I'm guilty of being an online social stalker; it started with just checking my significant other's timeline and mentions once or twice a month, and it grew into an every hour on the hour ritual. You know what they say, "when you look for something eventually you'll find what you've been looking for." My intuition and fear of not knowing, was what was driving my crazy obsession.

One thing you can count on when it comes to social networks is the other person making it apparent they're in the picture. Make no mistakes THIS IS NOT ACCIDENTAL. Even when he would try to assure me that it was innocent, it would be hard for me to believe because she would make it a point to be in his online mentions. Or even worse sending out subliminal tweets here and there…She was baiting me.

Be careful of the online bait and switch

As childish as it seems, a woman that is interested in your man will do this even if things are completely platonic between her and your significant other. She does this to cause friction between you and him in an effort to sabotage your relationship. While you're busy going crazy about a subliminal tweet or mention, she is trying to maneuver herself in, I have fallen victim to this trap.

Subliminal Tweet Examples:

How to Counteract: She is expecting you to send out sub-tweets and start mentioning him. DO ABSOLUTELY NOTHING. If you have a good man, he has already assured you and put you at ease about the whole situation. So just sit back…Better yet, try not to sign into your account for a few days or more, and if you do log into your account to sneak a peek, DO NOT UPDATE YOUR STATUS. This will keep her guessing; although you're a watcher; remember the watcher is being watched.

Now…when you finally log back into the social world, use the art of transference and transfer the energy by posting only positive updates and photos; this confuses her. There's nothing a woman enjoys more than victory over another woman, so don't let her tactics triumph over you, ***she may be a threat but you are your only opponent.***

If by chance your man is anything like my friend I mentioned earlier, then it is safe to say he gave the other woman reason enough to feel she can infringe. When a man cheats, we always blame the other woman and seldom "hold" the man responsible for the act. A blade inserted by another woman is fatal while a man's blade only gives us surface cuts— which is why we forgive a man's infidelity so quickly and hold the other woman accountable. Sadly, in our society a man's infidelity is expected and in most cases accepted. We rarely take into account that the other woman may not know anything about you. There's a huge chance that your significant other may have failed to mention his involvement with you to the other woman. The supposed "home-wrecker" may in fact be just as much of a victim as you are. So who's the actual enemy here, and how do you deal with the interference?

Go straight to the source of the problem; *to kill the weed you have to attack it at its roots*. Don't take the drama to the other woman, do not go to your girlfriends for advice or help on the situation, that will only add fuel to the fire, a mature woman knows when and how to cut the drama out of her life. Time is money, don't waste it on penniless thoughts; you can either deal with the problem directly or choose to move on.

"It really irks my nerves when people want to blame their relationship misfortunes on social media networks. NEWSFLASH! Twitter, Facebook nor Instagram didn't ruin your relationship. YOU ruined it because you forget that these sites were created for networking and staying connected with loved ones. Not for you to air out your laundry, or see how many statuses, pics and tweets your significant other has liked then turn around and get mad about it. Let's get it together." - Nellie Diamond facebook

"Emotions are treacherous and fleeting. Try not to make decisions solely based on them." – Joujou Paul facebook

HUMAN ROBOTS

We start our initial programming at a very young age, first in our homes by our parents and family, then through school, religion, friends, the mass media and so on and so on. We are the product of our environment; we are taught how to talk, walk and act -- what is deemed right and wrong -- we are soldiers in the army of conformity, the product of society's insecurities. Because of the desire and peer-pressure to "fit in," most people suppress their individual ideas and beliefs and choose to comply with the norm even if they disagree with the views and opinions of others. In our social environment, conformity has more to do with obedience, we are afraid that we will be chastised or criticized for our individual points of views and actions.

Unconformity and self-confidence are one and the same or should I say, one cannot be achieved without the other. When you're fully confident, you are less likely to care about what other people think or do; you follow your own lead. Social norms make it hard to break away from conformity. We are so caught up in the matrix that it's hard for us to short circuit the original hard wiring of our peers and reformat our own programming.

These conformities fall into both the relationships we have with ourselves and our significant others. We look to media outlets such as television programming, social networks, and even our social peers for guidance and more often than not, this commonly results in the blind leading the blind.

Some people are incapable of being in functional, real-life relationships, so they seek out the artificial online companionship thus eliminating the true notion of having a companion and being in a relationship. If only we could actually take a few scenes from the 1985 sci-fi film *Weird Science* -- and somehow build or create a perfect mate or relationship by inserting our computers with miscellaneous objects and photos. In reality, that option is not "*yet*" available, so for now we have to work at building relationships that are ideal for you and your significant other.

Fuck! Everyone's opinion of what 'your' relationship should be or look like. No two human beings are alike— therefore, no two relationships are alike. What works for Joe Blow and Jane Pretend may not work for you. There is no magic potion or hocus pocus when in a shaky relationship -- sometimes you just need to re-build and refocus. Focus on what you and your partner have in common and stop comparing your love life to what the media sets as guidelines. It seems there is no way around technology and social networks -- they say if you can't beat them, just join them. Join them but first create boundaries -- I know it's almost impossible to cut ties with the electronic world since it has become part of our evolution, but sometimes we have to disconnect to reconnect -- even if it's just for a little while.

"To go against the dominant thinking of your friends, of most of the people you see every day, is perhaps the most difficult act of heroism you can perform." - Theodore H. White

"By not caring too much about what people think, I'm able to think for myself and propagate ideas which are very often unpopular. And I succeed." - Albert Ellis

"In the age of information, ignorance is a choice" - Unknown facebook

The battle between social networks vs. social skills is upon us— in the end…who will win?

ABOUT THE AUTHOR

Although armed with a background in Fine Arts Claudia Versailles— dabbles in quite a few things. An event coordinator specializing in marketing and promotions— Interior Designing, CEO of F.A.K.E T-shirts, script writing, artist, art enthusiast, homeless advocate, dog lover, obsessed with Mike & Ike candy and a recovering social networks addict (she relapses from time to time)— shortly put— a renaissance woman . Claudia resides in Miami, Florida.

www.ingramcontent.com/pod-product-compliance
Lightning Source LLC
Chambersburg PA
CBHW071126280326
41935CB00010B/1127

* 9 7 8 0 9 8 9 1 6 7 2 0 8 *